CASTLE
A MASTER FILE
KEY STAGES 2 - 3

Compiled by

D. C. Perkins, BA (Hons), MEd, PhD (Wales) and E J Perkins, BSc (Hons), MEd

Illustrations by Craig Hildrew and Anthony James

MASTER FILES are planned for use in the classroom. Each consists of teachers' notes, pupils' resource material, worksheets, ideas for project work and assessment tables. Each book covers part of the National Curriculum in depth allowing the teacher to decide the amount of material to use according to the age and ability of the children.

DOMINO BOOKS (WALES) LTD
SWANSEA SA1 1FN
Tel. 01792 459378 Fax. 01792 466337

Castles Master File © EJP & DCP 1994. Reprinted 1995, 1996, 1997, 1998.
Revised and updated 1999.
ISBN 1 85772 075 X

CONTENTS

CASTLES

SOCIOLOGY
Class structure
Chivalry
The castle hierarchy
Feudalism
Society within castles
The position of nobles
The position of the
monarch
Women/men/boys/girls

ENGLISH
Castle vocabulary
Cloze test
Sequencing
Letter writing
Imaginative writing
A castle list
Writing a speech
Word search
Quiz

MATHEMATICS
Size and dimensions of
castles
Quantities of materials
used to build castles
Cost of building castles
Distances travelled
Coinage
Market prices

CASTLES CROSS-CURRICULAR LINKS AND ACTIVITIES

GEOGRAPHY
Geographical reasons for
the locations of castles
The position of towns that
grew from or near castles
Map work

COOKING
Medieval food
Medieval cooking
Food changes throughout
history
Cooking utensils

ART
Castle architects
Castle design
Castle building
Armour
Medieval art
Colours and shapes

SCIENCE
Type of materials used
to build castles
Warfare as a science
Sieges
Siege weapons
Defensive systems

TEACHERS' NOTES AND RESOURCES

HOW TO USE YOUR MASTER FILE

For many experienced teachers these few lines may seem superfluous. This book is planned to introduce pupils to British castles. The degree of difficulty varies throughout the book. Following the National Curriculum guidelines, it is especially helpful for those studying key stages 2 and 3 (but there is much to interest younger children at the beginning of their study of British history). Men have always built castles, to attack and to defend. Youngsters still play 'king of the castle'. We hope this book develops the fascination and awe we feel for these grand icons of the past and promotes an understanding of the part they have played in history.

1. All the material in this book is photocopiable as defined on page 1. This means that all the material can be used in any way you wish in the classroom situation. Drawings may be photocopied and adapted for further work.

2. Covering sections of the master copies with plain paper enables resource material to be used in different ways.

3. Reduction of the A4 master copies to A5 means that they can be pasted in children's exercise books. The master copies can also be enlarged to A3 to make it easier for students to work on them as a group.

4. Some of the photocopies can be cut up to make additional puzzles and games.

5. It is intended that material be used at different levels depending on the ages and abilities of your pupils.

6. It may be possible to use some of the Teachers' Notes directly with more advanced and brighter students.

7. Some of the worksheets and resources are more difficult than others and we do not envisage any problems with selecting appropriate material.

8. Some of the copy in the teachers' resources may be used in other ways, e.g. as cloze tests, sequencing exercises and so on.

9. Much of the completed work may be used as visual aids around the classroom.

10. Project work may be done individually, in groups and/or with teacher participation.

We hope you enjoy using this book and welcome any comments.

CHRONOLOGY OF CASTLES

It is important to establish a chronology of castles and to point out that strongholds of one sort or another have been with us since man learned to build. The emphasis here is on castles in Britain and reference should be made to the earliest defences erected: Bronze Age and Iron Age hillforts built a thousand years or more before Christ. There are approximately 2,500 of these on mainland Britain. Many of these early fortifications were very small but some such as Maiden Castle in Dorset are impressive and extensive. The brochs of northern Scotland and the Isles date from the same period. Gurness Broch in Orkney is a good example.

Roman forts and fortifications are very few. Roman walls do exist, however, at Porchester in Hampshire, Colchester in Essex, at Chester, at Lincoln, at Burgh Castle in Suffolk and at Caerleon in Gwent. But the best and most famous of our Roman heritage fortifications are Hadrian's Wall and the fort on the wall at Housesteads in Northumberland.

Little evidence remains of Anglo-Saxon fortresses although we know they fortified Bamburgh (Northumberland) and Tintagel in Cornwall.

Castle building began in earnest after the Norman Conquest. William the Conqueror, his sons and their Plantagenet successors were keen castle builders. Rochester, Ludlow, the Tower of London, Castle Hedingham, Lewes and Richmond all belong to this period. William's tenants-in-chief were also keen on castles.

Castle building reached its zenith in Wales in the 13th. century. Edward 1, eager to subdue the Welsh, built strongholds at Caerphilly in Gwent and Conwy, Beaumaris and Caernarfon in Gwynedd.

In the 14th. century castle building wavered as people began to want more comfortable dwellings. This was the time of fortified country houses such as Hever in Leeds and Penshurst in Kent.

But the age of the castle was not over. Henry VIII built castles as coastal defences and they were centres of conflict and intrigue throughout the 17th. century when royalists defended them against the Parliamentarians. Even in the early 18th. century in Scotland, the castle in Edinburgh withstood attack from the Young Pretender during the Jacobite rebellion.

In the 18th. and 19th. centuries the original martial use of castles declined and they were built for show. In the 20th. century the need for building new castles is questionable. Nowadays, medieval castles are preserved for posterity.

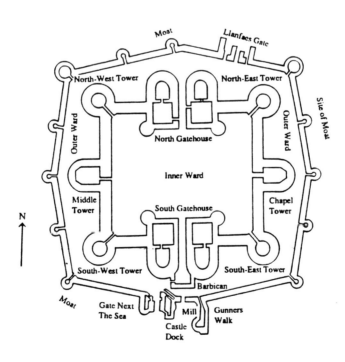

Beaumaris Castle - Ground Plan

CHRONOLOGY OF CASTLE DEVELOPMENT

3,000 BC   Rough Stone Age structures built with primitive tools.

2,000 BC   Bronze Age. Forts built on hills.

900 - 100 BC   Iron Age. Hillforts built designed mainly to protect tribes against attack. Many were small, built to defend farms and homesteads but some were extensive such as Maiden Castle in Dorset.

AD 43   Roman forts. Very few remain - Caerleon near Newport, Caer Gybi at Holyhead.
Roman walls at Colchester and Lincoln. Burgh Castle in Suffolk.
Most famous is Hadrian's Wall and the fort on the wall at Housesteads in Northumberland.

500 - 1000   Angles, Saxons and Danes invaded Britain. In 547 the Saxons fortified Bamburgh in Northumberland. Tintagel in Cornwall was also refortified in Anglo-Saxon times. But little evidence of these strongholds remains.

1066   Norman Conquest. First 'real' castles built.

11th century   Most were built of earth and wood - motte and bailey castles.

12th century   Earth and wood castles were replaced by stone ones. Norman castles were built at Rochester (Kent), Ludlow (Shropshire), the Tower (London), Castle Hedingham (Essex), Lewes (Sussex), Durham, Lincoln and Richmond (Yorkshire).
Henry II, his sons Richard I and John, and his grandson Henry III were all castle builders.

13th century   Stone keeps developed. Many ideas brought back from the Crusades were incorporated into British castles. Castle building in Wales reached its peak. De Clare's Caerphilly Castle in Gwent covering 12 hectares (30 acres) was the first of the concentric castles. It was followed by royal castles at Conwy, Beaumaris and Gwynedd. Concentric castles and walled towns were fully developed.

14th century   The need for strong defences gave way to the desire for more comfort. Castle building
&   changed into the construction of fortified country houses. The start of this process can be
15th century   seen in Hever, Leeds, Penshurst (Kent), Bodiam (Sussex) and Stokesay (Shropshire).

16th century   The Tudors, particularly Henry VIII, built a series of coastal defences as protection against European foes especially the French. The best examples are at Deal in Kent and Pendennis in Cornwall.

17th century   Medieval and other castles were used extensively in the Engish Civil War, 1642 - 1651. Royalist strongholds were *slighted* (i.e. destroyed) by the Parliamentarians to prevent them being used for military purposes. The last castle to surrender was Raglan in Gwent.

18th century   In Scotland castles were used in the Jacobite rebellions. Edinburgh held out against the Young Pretender in 1745. Country mansions developed. They were often called 'castles' for reasons of prestige or grandeur but were really large houses with fortifications.

19th century   The trend to build fortified mansions continued. Arundel and Alnwick were 'rebuilt' by fashionable architects (Wyatt and Salvin) to give them a martial appearance. Penrhyn in Gwynedd was created by a slate millionaire. Tennyson's grandfather built a castle at Tealby in Lincolnshire complete with portcullis, drawbridge and jousting arena. Cardiff Castle and Castell Coch in Glamorgan were also 'rebuilt' for prestige.
Shore defences were reinforced.

20th century   Some forts were reinforced for defence against Germany (1914 - 18 and 1939 - 45 World Wars). Pill boxes were also built and some of these still remain.

THE DEVELOPMENT OF CASTLES

Even the earliest men had to defend themselves from wild animals or opposing families and tribes. The history of castles and forts in Britain goes back to 3,000 BC when, in the Stone Age, fortified camps were built on hills for housing men and stabling cattle. They were constructed with bone or stone tools. In the Bronze Age (about 2,000 BC) more hilltop forts were built and in the Iron Age (900 - 100 BC) these forts were rebuilt or extended. Mainly anti-invasion strongholds, over 2,500 existed throughout the United Kingdon.

During Roman times, the whole of Britain was occupied. The Romans were famous for roads and baths but they also had garrisons of soldiers billetted in forts. An example of this in Wales is Caerleon. One of the largest of the Roman inland forts, manned by well trained auxiliaries was Y Gaer, the Roman fort at Brecon.

From the 4th. to the 10th. centuries Britain was in a state of turmoil. Danes, Saxons and Angles invaded in turn and to protect themselves, people built earthworks especially around large villages and towns.

The great Norman warrior king, William the Conqueror, siezed England at the Battle of Hastings in 1066. He knew the value of castles.

A castle was a home - but it was also well protected - a fortress where people and animals were safe from attack. Castles were now built to defend vital places such as (i) a town, (ii) a river crossing, (iii) a port, (iv) important cross roads, (v) gaps through hills, (vi) the coast, (vii) a border or (viii) simply to defend places already won in battle.

After the Norman Conquest, William permitted castles to be built wherever they were needed to protect a strategic interest and to maintain control over the natives. Such castles were built by tenants-in-chief, followers of the Conqueror.

MOTTE AND BAILEY CASTLES

The early Norman strongholds were very simple and are known as motte and bailey castles. They consisted of a motte - a natural or artificial mound of earth - on which a wooden tower or keep was built. Most mottes were 10 - 12 metres high and were surrounded by a ditch or moat.

The motte was connected to a large outer enclosure or courtyard called a bailey. This was protected by its own ditch, moat or bank and was surrounded by a timber fence of stakes or palisade. Domestic buildings were usually placed in the bailey (e.g. the kitchens) because of the risk of fire.

A castle of this type could be constructed in a matter of weeks and when attacked, the garrison could retreat into the motte and hold out until relief arrived. All mottes had one special feature, there was no door on the ground floor. Access into a castle was always gained via an opening at first floor level and entry was by a ladder or a light footbridge which could be withdrawn in the event of a surprise attack.

STONE SHELL KEEPS

Motte and bailey castles were fairly easy to capture or set alight because they were made of wood and quickly fired. Stone came to be used instead of wood and shell keep castles emerged. These were a natural development of the earlier strongholds, a stone wall replacing the wooden stakes or palisade on top of the motte. Buildings were then erected inside the shell and these included a hall, a solar (or study), a chapel and a kitchen.

Square stone keeps were eventually built bigger and stronger. They were often up to 35 metres high, and were erected in three or four storeys with spiral staircases in the corner turrets. As the size and weight of these keeps grew, they were built on natural hills or more often on flat ground.

A typical stone keep had a basement with three storeys. The basement was for stores and prisoners, soldiers were garrisoned on the first floor, the Great Hall and the Lord's solar were on the second floor, and sleeping rooms were on the third. Roof and battlements were above. The windows were thin slits in the brickwork, just wide enough to let chinks of light in and ideal for firing arrows through at anyone daring to attack the stronghold.

Some strongholds were rectangular stone towers and these dominated the castle scene until the end of the 11th. century. To defend themselves against intruders, a series of additions were eventually made to these stone castles. These adaptations included:

1. A forebuilding to protect the castle entrance.
2. A plinth (a rectangular slab or block of stone) to stop battering rams reaching the bottom of the walls.
3. The development of circular keeps. Rectangular keeps wih their corners meant that the enemy could not always be seen. Therefore, circular or multiangular towers were built which gave no cover to the enemy at any point.

CONCENTRIC CASTLES

In the 13th. century (about 1250) a type of castle new to Britain emerged. These new castles owed much to those built in the Byzantine Empire and at the time of the Crusades. (It must be remembered that many ideas

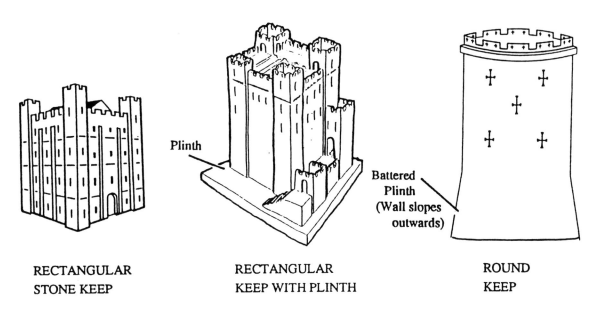

| RECTANGULAR STONE KEEP | RECTANGULAR KEEP WITH PLINTH | ROUND KEEP |

DEVELOPMENT OF THE STONE KEEP

about castle construction had been used by the Egyptians 2000 years before the birth of Christ.) Basically, the plan was to build outer walls or a series of walls. Such castles were often concentric castles. (Their defences were in rings with the same centre.)

Many built in Wales by Edward 1 were of this type. They had two sets of defensive walls (called curtain walls) and if intruders broke through the outer curtain, they still had to attack the inner one. Attackers were trapped between the two sets of walls. Beaumaris is a typical Welsh concentric castle.

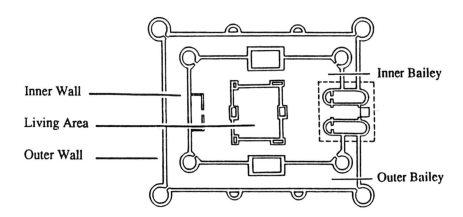

PLAN OF A CONCENTRIC CASTLE

A central keep eventually became a thing of the past. Instead, concentric castles had large inner baileys and people lived in dwellings built against the walls. Thus, castle developments by this time included:

1. A strong wall called a curtain built around the living area.
2. The division of the castle into two sections, the inner bailey and the outer bailey. The living area stood in the inner bailey, a courtyard where the kitchen, granary and other storerooms were found. Beyond was the outer bailey, a large enclosure containing domestic buldings, stables, gardens and a training and exercise area.
3. Further protection of the outer bailey by high walls, D-shaped and round towers, a gatehouse, drawbridge and moat.

Typical concentric castles include Warwick, the Tower of London, Beaumaris, Conwy and Harlech.

CASTLE DEFENCES

Although medieval castles differ greatly they were all designed to protect those who lived within them: safety from attack, especially surprise attack, was a major consideration. Defensive structures included the following:

THE SITE This was often chosen so that there were natural advantages which helped to protect it. Natural defences included (a) an elevated position such as on a hill, (b) the sea on one side so that a potential enemy would have to cross water, (c) a river on one side again offering the protection of water, (d) an open view so that enemies could be seen as they approached.

THE MOATS These were stretches of water or deep ditches below the castle walls. These wet or dry defences stopped the enemy from reaching the walls and discouraged scaling them. They also hampered those who tried to destroy the walls by digging at their bases.

THE CASTLE WALLS These were built as thick as possible to withstand attack.
Curtain walls are a good example and were often the main defensive structure. The stone used in some castles was imported from Caen in Normandy. The thickness of the walls varied from castle to castle and averaged 2 to 3 metres (6 to 9 feet). Caernarfon Castle in North Wales has a curtain wall 5 metres (15 feet) thick. Many walls had **wall walks** - thick at the top so that men-at-arms could patrol along them and survey the approaches to the stronghold.
Battlements These were designed to allow archers to defend them. They were able to fire through the openings, called crenels, while shielding themselves behind the sections sticking up called merlons.
Shutters These were wooden (later iron) shutters which fitted between the merlons at the top. The bottom of these could be pushed outwards to allow archers to fire on the enemy then they dropped back into place as a protective guard against enemy missiles.
Hourdes These were covered platforms fixed to castle walls. Holes in the floors of the platforms allowed missiles (stones, sand, dead carcasses and other materials) to be dropped on the enemy at the base of the castle walls. First, they consisted of temporary wooden structures built at the top of the curtain walls. Later, such hourdes were made of masonry covered with slates and were permanent.
Machiocolations These were similar to hourdes and made of stone.
Arrow loops These were openings in the walls from which archers could fire. Inside, they were wide enough to give an archer a clear field of vision and adequate room to manoeuvre. On the outside of the wall they were mere fissures so that the enemy could not hit defenders through them.
Square towers This shape gave protection to archers who would otherwise have had to lean out to see the bottom of the walls.
Round towers These were soon preferred to square ones. Castle defenders had a clearer field of vision, missiles glanced off the walls more readily. Round towers were less vulnerable to attack: they did not collapse so easily as square towers when the enemy dug at the base of their walls.
Plinths These structures consisted of extra stone to strengthen the bottom of the walls. They also provided a slope difficult to climb and on to which missiles could be dropped from above. The missiles then bounced off in the direction of the enemy.

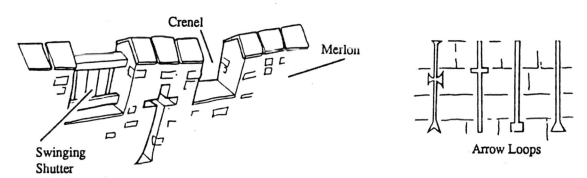

DEFENSIVE STRUCTURE OF THE CURTAIN WALL

POSTERN This was a small door at the back of the castle through which individuals (especially important ones) could escape.

THE ENTRANCE This was the most vulnerable part of a castle and an enemy often tried to gain access

through it. The entrance was protected by several defensive structures:-

The drawbridge This spanned the moat or ditch in front of the entrance. Made of wood, it was raised to prevent access to the castle door. Usually, it was hinged at the side of the castle and was pulled up on chains attached to a windlass in the floor above the entrance. Holes through the walls allowed access for the chains.

The gatehouse This structure projected from the walls. Usually there were arrow loops on either side of the door.

The portcullis This was a strong grating made of oak, plated and shod wih iron, which could be moved up and down in stone grooves. It blocked entry to the door of the castle.

The wooden door This was made of very heavy wood reinforced by a drawbar.

Gate passage From the portcullis and door, a narrow passageway led into the castle. This passage had holes (murder holes) in the ceiling which could be used for dropping sand, stones, firebrands and similar missiles on to intruders. There were also arrow loops in the side walls. There might also be another portcullis and door at the other end of the passage. If the outer door was closed after the enemy had gained access to the passage, they were trapped in the passage between the doors.

Murder holes These holes in the gate and ceiling were used to attack the enemy. They could also be used to put out fires lit by the enemy to burn the door/s.

The barbican To protect the gatehouse and entrance to the castle, a walled outwork was often built in front of it. This was called the barbican and was an enclosure with one or two towers and a whole system of defences. Often it was a dual defence system, the barbican and gatehouse having the same arrangement. If the enemy entered the barbican, close-set parallel walls with towers slowed them down and they became easy targets for arrow-fire from above. Sometimes the enemy were deliberately allowed to get through the barbican. Both sides were then closed trapping the besiegers.

LATER CASTLES

ARROW LOOP WITH THE
ADDITION OF A GUN LOOP
FOR FIRING CANNON

By the end of the 15th. century, siege warfare involving castles declined. Gunpowder had been invented and walls could be more easily breached. Gun loops began to appear in castle walls: holes to fire cannon were often cut below arrow slits. Differences of opinion began to be settled on the open battlefield. The Welshman, Henry VII, for example, defeated Richard III at Bosworth Field (1485).

Wealthy people began to live in manor houses. But there was still a need for castles. Henry VII and VIII annoyed the French from time to time and there was every possibility of invasion from across the Channel. Thus, coastal castles were built against invasion and many of the old castles repaired. Henry VIII in particular built a series of artillery forts (at Walmer, Deal, Cumber, St. Mawes and Pendennis) to offer resistance to the enemy. They carried on the idea of the concentric castle but increased the number of deflecting surfaces.

It is sometimes thought that by the end of the 15th. century, traditional castles had outlived their usefulness. But this is untrue. The strength of medieval walls against gunfire was proved in the English Civil War (1642 - 1651) for many old castles could not be captured even by crack troops with the latest 17th. century artillery. Again, when Napoleon threatened in the 18th. and early 19th. centuries, coastal defences including ancient castles were reinforced to rebuff him. New structures called Martello towers were erected. When Adolf Hitler presented a similar threat in 1940 another programme of up-dating defences was begun, the British army used many of Henry VIII's castles effectively.

In the 19th. and 20th centuries, castles were of four types. Some buildings called castles were in reality fortified manor houses, some medieval castles were made more comfortable to live in, e.g. Manorbier Castle in Dyfed, while others were rebuilt often on a medieval site for prestige, e.g. Cardiff Castle and Castell Coch, Tongwynlais near Cardiff. Then there were 'show' castles with military features designed to impress.

SUMMARY OF
CASTLE DEVELOPMENT

3,000 BC
Rough Stone Age structures.

2,000 BC
Bronze Age forts on hills.

900 - 100 BC
Iron Age forts often developed from earlier buildings.

AD 43
Roman forts built after invasion and occupation.

500 - 1,000
Danes, Angles and Saxons invade.
Towns fortified against attack.

1066
Norman Conquest. Many motte and bailey castles speedily built.

11th century
Wooden castles (some already being built of stone).

12 - 13th centuries
More stone castles built. Development of stone keeps.
Many ideas brought back from the Crusades in the Middle East incorporated into the new castles.
Castles built with perimeter walls. A second perimeter wall also built - concentric castles.

14th century
Further development of concentric castles and walled towns.

15th century
Return to more basic, simple castle structures: comfort the keynote.
Show 'castles' and manor houses developed.

16th century
Tudors built shore forts for protection especially against the French.

17th century
Medieval castles used in the Civil War 1642 - 1651. Many 'slighted' (destroyed) after the war.

18th century
Country mansions developed. Some were 'prestige' buildings.

19th century
Many shore forts - Martello towers built - in case of a Napoleonic invasion.
Reinforcement of shore defences.
Some castles built by the wealthy (fortified manor houses) or added to for prestige.

20th century
Shore forts reinforced for defence against Germany (1914 - 18 and 1939 - 45 World Wars).
Pill boxes also built and some of these still remain.

CASTLES IN VARIOUS MODES

For most of the year a medieval castle was a quiet place with few staff. Every so often it might be visited by a monarch or one of his tenants-in-chief (nobles). It was then that the castle became a very different place. A lord and lady were accompanied by an extensive entourage of knights, senior members of the household, numerous servants and hundreds of horses. This is how the great households spent their time, constantly on the move and one historian has estimated that the important nobles moved on average about once a month throughout the year.

When the monoarch or nobles arrived, the medieval castle became a place for feasting, hunting and having fun. When they left, the castle returned to its peaceful existence.

PERSONNEL IN A MEDIEVAL CASTLE

The Lord and Lady These were the most important people in the castle and the whole organisation depended on them. They were looked after by senior members of the household who were also nobility or gentry. (See next page.)

The Constable or Castellan was the official in charge of the resident staff. He was responsible for castle security and supervised any military staff on the premises and always stayed at the castle. He also supervised permanent servants such as the porter, gaoler and watchmen.

The Steward or Seneschal was a key official when the royal or baronial party arrived. He was responsible for the organisation of the meals of the household in the main eating place (the Great Hall). This gave him responsibility for the kitchens and the estates which supplied the food. By the 13th century, many large household had two stewards, one to control the estates and one who dealt with household food.

The Marshal was responsible for all household travel arrangements and **all servants outdoors**. These included grooms and blacksmiths, kennel men and falconers, cart makers, armourers and fletchers (arrow makers). He was also responsible for arranging sporting activities such as deer or boar hunting and hawking.

The Chamberlain cared for the bedroom or chamber of the head of the household. He was in charge of the lord's clothing and bathing. He also had responsibility for household valuables.

The Chancellor or Chaplain was in charge of the clergy and places of worship. He surpervised the work of the church and said mass. He was responsible for all secretarial duties because in the early middle ages, church ministers were the only people who could read and write.

The Treasurer or Wardrober was responsible for the accounts. He kept the money which came into the household, paid the bills and monitored the accounts. He had his own office with clerks who counted money on a chequered board.

The Almoner Most medieval households employed a number of clerks to look after day-to-day affairs. One of these clerks was the almoner responsible for dispensing any food left over to the poor. He also passed on cast-off clothes.

Knights A castle garrison usually included these men who had to provide military service to the owner of the castle. The 'castle guard' was part of the feudal relationship.

Reeve Such an official was the local representative of the owner of the castle. He was responsible for the manors, market places and courts which the baron owned. He collected all rents, market fees and court fines and was supervised by the seneschal of the lands.

Armourer This was an important position for he looked after the stocks of weapons and armour. Such equipment as bows, bow-strings, bolts, arrows, helmets and swords came within his care. He repaired armour and kept this and weapons free from rust by cleaning them with sand and vinegar. He also sharpened swords and was sometimes able to advise on larger weapons such as siege weapons.

The Butler was concerned with buying, storing and serving wine.

The Household As well as the main officials, a castle had a variety of other servants including huntsmen, falconers, grooms, smiths, masons and carpenters whilst there might be a fruiterer, a porter of the royal bed and a keeper of the tents. A castle was a very busy place with most people working from dawn until dusk: fetching water, wood for fuel, grooming horses, washing and mending clothes, brewing ale, baking bread, and all the daily chores necessary in a self sufficient community. A priest said morning prayers and taught the pages. Every boy had regular training in the use of weapons. The lady of the castle or an apothecary helped to make ointments and care for the sick.

Catering was the major concern and many servants were employed to prepare and serve food. Sheep and pigs were kept for meat, chickens, geese and swans were also reared for meat and eggs while cows and goats provided mlk. The cook was regarded as a servant of some distinction and was paid more than other workers. Those attached to the pantry and buttery were responsible for serving food and drink.

Castle servants were well thought of and all were paid and had their clothes and board and lodging provided.

LORDS AND LADIES

These were the most important people in a castle. Usually they visited particular places for only a few weeks at a time but whilst on a visit they were looked after constantly. Until the 14th century most lords and ladies spoke French while the lower classes spoke English. Most marriages between lords and ladies were business transactions arranged by their families or the monarch. Men usually married women younger than themselves. The baron commanded knights, as few as a dozen or as many as fifty. The knights were served by pages and squires, boys and young men usually of noble birth being trained to become knights.

The barons usually had castles and estates in different parts of the country. When they visited them, they found out what was going on and kept tight control over their lands and subjects. They could also collect taxes and dues, hold courts to give orders and arrange trials to punish transgressors. Near a castle, were dwellings belonging to the lord. People living in these were obliged to provide food and servants. It was often difficult to supply enough. Orders would go out to the people requiring them to provide flour for bread; cows and goats for milk; pigs, sheep and cattle for meat; hens, ducks and swans for eggs. As well, hay was needed for the horses.

BOYS AND GIRLS

Most royal parents and nobles saw little of their offspring when they were very young. Little children were looked after by wet-nurses. Later they were sent to another castle or household to learn manners. Boys and girls born to noble families had special rights and responsiblities and a role in the castle where they had been sent. In the early middle ages, there was no formal education for either boys or girls. Children often died young. **Boys** were favoured because succession fell upon them. They were often placed in a neighbouring baron's household where they might train as pages who served one or even two knights. They began their day by helping their masters to dress. After breakfast they would be taught reading, writing and Latin by one of the chaplain's priests. These classes might be followed by singing and dancing classes. They practised fighting with light wooden swords and might also help with hunting and hawking activities. When they were older, boys usually became knights' squires. They then had to learn to ride war-horses and use adult swords and lances. Eventually, they became knights, a highly regarded profession.

Boys who did not train for military life might be sent to an abbey or cathedral school to be trained to become priests or for administrative and clerical work. They could become officials at the king's court or lawyers or officials in the law courts.

Girls had two choices, they could either marry or become nuns. Girls were often betrothed at a very young age. Most were married by the time they were thirteen. Joan was probably only ten when she married Llywelyn the Great and Margaret Beaufort was only thirteen when she gave birth to the future King Henry VII at Pembroke Castle. Girls were taught by nuns - how to be a lady-in-waiting or how to be a good wife for a baron. In the later middle ages, the daughter of a noble would probably be taught to read and write and learn to dance, sing and embroider. Marriage was for life in England but couples could separate in Wales. A wife could leave her husband if he became ill. After seven years of marriage, the belongings were divided equally between them. Traditionally, the husband claimed the oldest and youngest sons and the wife kept the middle one.

If a young girl did not want to marry or no one wanted to marry her, then she could choose between a number of nunneries throughout the country. Girls entered the nunneries when they were very young.

A noblewoman had to look after a large household. She had to instruct staff, organise meals and manage the budget. The size and structure of the kitchen , the number of people to be fed and the variety of the menus required by tradition to satisfy the status of the diners made preparing meals difficult and time consuming. A widow of a noble was allowed to keep a third of her dead husband's estate for the rest of her life.

A craftsman's wife was expected to help him at his work although she was paid about half as much as he was for the same work. Similarly, a farmer's wife worked in the fields, milked the cows, made butter and cheese, baked and cooked and looked after the children. Families tended to be large because so many babies and young children died. Less is known about women in medieval times than about their men folk. It seems that those women who were able to write had little time for making written records.

COOKING

In early castles food was prepared in a wooden shed in a courtyard. Later castles had kitchens. Much of the meat (venison, boars, hares and rabbits) was roasted on fixed metal rods called spits above the kitchen fire or open hearth. A servant boy was employed to turn these spits so that the meat roasted evenly. There was no butter and fat dripping from the meat was precious and as much as possible was caught in bowls. Large bronze cooking pots called cauldrons were used to cook soups while bread was baked in an oven at the back or near the open hearth. Spices and herbs were used extensively. Without refrigeration, food, especially meat, often went bad. In the summer, the household lived well and many courses would be carried to the Great Hall by servants and served by squires. The dishes included chicken and squirrel broth, salmon with orange, trout with

spices, shellfish scented with herbs, sugared mackerel, roasted swan or venison, boar's head with brawn, roast beef with chopped herbs, blancmange (a savoury dish in these times), stuffed quarter of bear, fresh fruit tarts, fig pudding, apple dumplings, cakes with honey and roasted chestnuts or nuts. Some kitchens were large enough to roast two or three oxen at the same time and unusual dishes such as dolphin, heron and peacock might be served. Sometimes, especially in winter, food was scarce and even the wealthy were forced to live on meagre rations such as beans and gruel (a thin porridge).

EATING

In the early Middle Ages, the main meals were eaten in the Great Hall which was regarded as the communal centre of the castle. Only the baron, his wife and special guests had chairs. These were arranged around a raised table, the high table which was served first. The other tables were just boards on trestles around which were benches. (These were cleared away after a meal to make room for other activities.) Everyone who lived in the castle ate together. Feast nights began at 5 pm and lasted for hours with often six to eight meat courses and over twenty dishes for each course. Squires served the 'top table' and pages served the lower tables. The baron and his family and his special guests may have eaten from pewter plates and had knives and spoons (there were no forks) but most people ate with their fingers, throwing scraps and bones on to the floor where dogs devoured them. Most of those eating shared dishes with a neighbour, only those on the high table could expect a dish for themselves. Generally, food was served on huge slabs of bread called trenchers. Those on the top table drank wine out of pewter goblets, whilst the servants, journeymen and apprentices drank ale or cider from clay mugs. Food from one trencher was usually shared by two people and people also shared goblets and mugs. The kind of foods eaten depended on the church calendar and the days of the week. No meat was eaten during Lent and there was a diet of fish and no meat on Fridays.

By the middle of the 14th century, dining with the whole household in the Great Hall declined and by the late Middle Ages, it was usual for the lord and lady to eat in private. The Great Hall might be used on feast days or when there were special guests.

WASHING

Water was very precious in the Middle Ages and often had to be carried from wells or rivers by servants. People, especially the lower classes, were not able to wash often. Soap was rare and people merely splashed themselves with water. The baron and his family used soap made of mutton fat, wood ash and soda. Men imagined that bathing reduced their strength and bathed rarely. The bath was a large wooden chest or barrel and bathing was something of an event. Water had to be heated and carried by the servants. The soap was soft and evil smelling so herbs and flowers were sprinkled on the water. The baron's wife bathed in the water first and then the other women took their turn. People did not clean their teeth and most suffered in later life from toothache and tooth decay. Until 1400, surgeon barbers believed in extracting only loose teeth and relied on crude instruments for carrying out such operations.

Royalty washed regularly. Henry I employed a 'ewerer' who organised the king's baths and provided water at mealtimes. King John took a bath once a fortnight and employed a bathman to provide his water. Later kings had more elaborate, often permanent, baths.

Even the earliest castles were provided with garderobes (toilets), usually holes in the walls with long chutes taking the waste into ditches or pits. Garderobes were often shared by a whole garrison although the baron and his family usually had their own. The principal bedchamber on the second floor of some castles had their own ensuite garderobes. But there were no disinfectants!

HEATING AND LIGHTING

Medieval castles were cold, damp and badly lit. In early castles the main heat came from a central hearth with a louvered opening in the roof through which smoke escaped. Light at night came from rushes or candles. When castles were made of wood fire was a serious risk. Private rooms were available for only a few castle dwellers: fireplaces appeared in these from the 13th century.

SLEEPING

At night, most people slept in the Great Hall, usually on the floor. Many had mattresses stuffed with straw and feathers which could be rolled up out of the way in daytime. Others slept on rushes. People usually slept in their day clothes and when they woke up they were dressed and ready for work. The baron and his wife were the only people to have their own rooms situated on the floor above the great hall. One of these rooms was the bed chamber. The bed was a valuable possession and usually travelled with them on their journeys. It had a wooden frame with a mattress on top. It was surrounded by curtains giving some privacy and protection from draughts and the cold. Several of the baron's servants slept in the same room as well as his children and dogs.

KNIGHTS AND ARMOUR

A knight in armour conjures up a romantic picture of life in the Middle Ages. It seems as if there was always something to fight about from land to the honour of a maiden. Much of the fighting in castles was done man to man and armour was developed to protect men from their foes. A knight was an armoured horse-soldier known as a 'man-at-arms'. Armour changed constantly throughout medieval times. The earliest suits were a coat of mail with a shield and iron helmet. These were gradually replaced by pieces of 'plate armour', a protective iron shell, until by the 15th. century, the knight was completely encased in iron. The mail protected the most vulnerable parts of the body. The weight of these suits became a problem. A knight sometimes became very hot and tired, and some died of heat stroke during a long battle. Armour became so cumbersome that when a knight fell down, it was difficult for him to get up. Encased in armour, all knights looked the same. Because of this a method of picture writing developed. These were special designs on a shield or armour which identified a knight or his lord. Such pictures were the personal heraldic coats of arms of a leader.

TOURNAMENTS, MÈLEES AND JOUSTS
The first tournaments started in France before the 12th century. They were intended to be training for cavalry engagements and were close to real warfare. Teams of knights fought bitterly until one side gave in and prisoners were taken. A battle of this type became known as a mêlée. Knights liked to take part for the glory and the cash that came from ransoming prisoners. By the reign of Henry I, tournaments had became popular in Britain. They were condemned by the Church but nevertheless young, ambitious knights continued to take part in them. From time to time, sovereigns banned them (Henry II for example) but Richard I used them to improve military capabilities. Whilst Henry III disapproved of them, his son Edward I, took part in them personally. The popularity of tournaments encouraged the growing art of heraldry and the attitude towards knighthood and chivalry.

By the end of the 14th century, one-to-one jousting became more important replacing the chaos of the mêlée. Tournaments became a day's programme of jousts in which knights participated in turn. Two knights on horseback charged at each other with long lances and tried to knock each other to the ground. In between them was a wooden barrier called a tilt which stopped the horses crashing into each other. There were three rounds. If nobody was unseated by the first charge, they turned and rode at each other with lances again. Finally, they fought each other on foot with swords until one of the knights fell on his knees or lost his sword. To prepare for a tournament or joust, young squires often practised riding at a 'quintain', a target with a weight attached which would swing and hit a rider who did not move out of the way quickly enough. War-horses were valuable commodities and cost about two years' pay. They were never used to hunt or to carry goods. When knights moved from place to place, they rode smaller horses called palfreys.

COATS OF ARMS
Before a joust, a knight wore a loose garment on the upper part of his body decorated with his personal insignia. That was how the phrase 'coat of arms' originated. The earliest known coat of arms was that of Geoffrey of Anjou who when knighted by his father-in-law, Henry I of England, received a shield decorated with lions from the King. Many shields incorporated lions, crowns, castles, animals and keys on the front: symbols of strength, bravery, power or possession. The Prince of Wales coat of arms is the well known - Ich dien. These insignia were most important at tournaments, mêlées and jousts. A knight not only had badges on his own person but dressed his page and horse in the same insignia. It was usual to put the insignia on banners outside his tent. The **herald** in charge of the tournament announced the names for each joust and could identify the badges of those taking part.

In 1484 the king appointed a College of Heralds to lay down strict conditions about the arms people could use and what they could display on them. This College still exists today.

OTHER PASTIMES, GAMES AND AMUSEMENTS
Favourite sports of these times included hunting for hares, rabbits and boars with deer being the preserve of the King or nobility. In falconry, peregrines, eagles and goshawks were trained to attack and bring back prey such as hares or rabbits or other birds.

'Bandy ball' was a very rough type of hockey in which a player was allowed to hit his opponent with a stick. There was also a form of tennis in which the ball was hit by the palm of the hand instead of a racquet. In winter, skating on ice with iron skates was popular. Indoors, chess was a favourite and dice were much used in gambling. Few people owned books because they had to be written by hand and few could read, but story telling was a much enjoyed pastime, especially swapping jokes together with singing and dancing. In large castles, there might be entertainment by a harpist or minstrels and sometimes jugglers and acrobats were hired to entertain special guests.

HERALDRY

Heraldry is the study of coats of arms and shields. The knights chose their own design and patterns (called 'devices') on their shields and many chose these to suit their name or the job they did, e.g. a trumpeter might have two or more trumpets on his shield. De Lucy, a fisherman had four luces (fish) on his shield. A shield may be divided in many ways. Here are a few with their names.

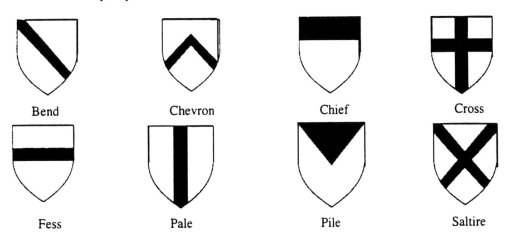

Bend	Chevron	Chief	Cross
Fess	Pale	Pile	Saltire

The main colours used in heraldry are: azure - blue, gales - red, purpure - purple, vert - green and sable - black.

Noble families in England have their own coats of arms. Below is the Coat of Arms of the Duke of Marlborough. There is a little shield within the big shield.

Coat of Arms of the Duke of Marlborough.

The little shield is called an 'augmentation' and is a great honour only given by the monarch to certain distinguished families. Only three noble families in England have such an augmentation: the Dukes of Wellington, the Dukes of Marlborough and the Dukes of Norfolk.

A NOTE ON TITLES AND PEERAGES

There are five ranks of English peer:
1st. Dukes
2nd. Marquesses
3rd. Earls
4th. Viscounts
5th. Barons (the lowest rank)

CHIVALRY AND FEUDALISM

CHIVALRY

In the Middle Ages the two words chivalry and feudalism governed the relationship between certain classes. The chivalric ethic was a loose set of principles which changed over a period of time. It was essentially the ways in which the warrior classes, the people who lived in castles, behaved towards each other and so it was intimately connected to kinghts and knighthood. The principles involved in chivalric behaviour included the following:

(i) It was dishonourable to attack an opponent who had no defence.

(ii) It was dishonourable for a knight or noble to attack the Lord's anointed, i.e. the King.

(iii) Knights duelling should avoid slaying each other but should take the vanquished knight captive.

(iv) Ceremonial associated with becoming a knight, called dubbing, should be undertaken.

(v) Knights should show respect to the weaker sex, women.

FEUDALISM

After his vistory at the Battle of Hastings, William the Conqueror brought in feudalism. This system was based on the principle that all land belonged to him. The King granted the use of it to tenants-in-chiefs for specific services. In turn, they required services and duties from their subjects and servants: thus all classes of society were bound together for mutual services and protection. Feudalism can, in a real sense, be compared to a pyramid where each man is tied to his superior and ultimately to the King.

Castles in war and peace operated within this feudal system. In return for their lands, the tenants-in-chief agreed to provide knights for the monarch's wars and for garrisoning his castles. The knights were given the use of land by the tenants-in-chief in return for this military service.

This feudal system dictated relationships at every level of medieval society. For example, frankalmoin was a feudal tenure peculiar to the church concerned with saying prayers or looking after a chantry while serjeanty covered a wide range of tenures in return for service and domestic work.

ATTACK

In the Middle Ages, castles had a two-fold purpose. They were centres from which attacks on enemies could be planned and mounted and havens to which the attackers could retreat. They were also places which could be defended against attack. How were castles attacked by an enemy?

BESIEGING This was the most popular method but it tended to take too long. The aim was to starve those inside into submission. This meant constant vigil so that no one could leave the castle or enter it. Attackers had to have a plentiful supply of food and water themselves.

SCALING THE WALLS Ladders, ropes, grappling irons and specially built seige towers were used. The castle had to be on a level site and not surrounded by moats and ditches.

DAMAGING WALLS AND TOWERS by various means so that attackers could gain entry. Numerous methods and devices were used. (See below).

BY STEALTH including using someone inside the castle as a spy who could let down the drawbridge or open the back door (the postern) allowing attackers to gain entry.

Many methods of attack were used simultaneously and a direct assault by a large number of men was often attempted. Often attacks were mounted at night under cover of darkness. The attacking force usually outnumbered the castle garrison and usually tried to scale the walls. Archers within and without would also be employed. They used two weapons - the longbow, a light weapon often as tall as the archer, and the crossbow. The latter was a mechanical weapon which could hurl an iron bolt accurately 300 to 400 metres.

The following notes give some indication of the methods used.

Siege Weapons

Castle walls and towers could be weakened by a constant barrage of small boulders, heavy stones, missiles or iron bolts.

Catapults
Straps usually made of leather under considerable torsion could hurl a 25kg weight a distance of 440 metres.

The Mangonel
This was one of the earliest of the catapults used in the reign of King Stephen (1135 - 1154). It had a range of about 200 metres and could fling boulders weighing about 25kg. It was especially useful if there was a moat. It could also hurl other missiles such as putrid carcasses and firebrands.

Trebuchet
This was a type of catapult with a large weight in front to counterbalance the tension in the sling. It could hurl objects 150 - 200 kg in weight over a distance of 600 metres. Later than the mangonel, it was probably first used in the time of King Henry II (1154 - 1189). It was used for a variety of purposes including hurling stones at castle walls and for propelling dead and diseased animals and burning material (Greek fire) over the walls into the castle. Stones hitting inside walls caused havoc because they shattered into fragments rather like shrapnel.

The Scorpion
This catapult was less powerful than the mangonel or trebuchet. It was useful, however, because it could be assembled on the spot.

The Ballista
The ballista or perrier was a smaller weapon. Essentially, it was a cross-bow fitted to a permanent stand. It was designed to fire bolts or small shot directly at the enemy. It was usually used against men and archers rather than against gatehouses or castle walls. The design of the ballista followed closely that of the cross-bow because it had a groove running down its middle where the projectile was placed for firing.

The Great Pivoting Crossbow
This was mounted on a three-wheeled carriage and could fire a boar-spear 5 metres long (known as a 'garrot') over a distance of 50 metres. It was most effective against infantry and cavalry sent out to combat an army besieging a castle.

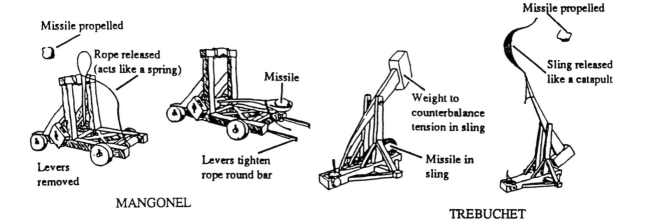

MANGONEL

TREBUCHET

The Belfry or Siege Tower
Mounted on wheels, a siege tower consisted of a ladder and an attacking platform. The tower (more than one may have been used at a time) was pushed against the castle wall. This enabled attackers to fight directly with the castle defenders. At the base was a compartment which sheltered the attackers during the approach to the castle. The attackers scaled ladders to reach the platform. The belfry also had devices for throwing missiles such as stones and dead carcasses over castle walls.

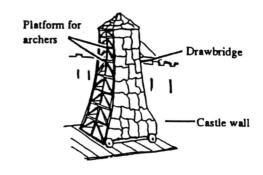

BELFRY

The Battering Ram

This was an iron-tipped tree trunk carried within a protective covering, a wagon-like structure on wheels. It was operated by 10 or 12 men, depending on its size and was slung from ropes. They reached the gate or wall and swung the ram backwards and forwards so as to set up a formidable pendulum-like movement which had considerable destructive power.

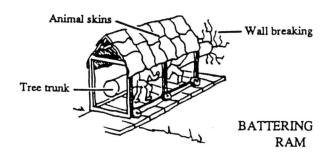

The Bore

This device was lighter than a ram and had a more pointed metal tip used to dislodge stones in the castle walls. Like the ram, men using the bore were protected by the same kind of covering called a pentise.

Attackers found it very difficult to approach castle walls and devised a number of ingenious ways of doing so. These included sapping and mining.

Sapping

After advancing along an open trench, under camouflage, the sappers loosened several stones of the outer wall of the castle. They then dug out the rubble inside. Once entry was achieved, the wall was shored up with props. Faggots covered with lard were piled in the hole in the wall and set alight. This method of attack known as mining with firebrands caused the wall to collapse at that point. (The debris usually fell into the moat making a bridge for attackers to cross.) Sapping took place **above** ground.

Mining

More complicated than sapping, those employed in this operation were skilled men who in peace time tunnelled into hillsides for lead, copper or tin. Mining a castle involved digging a mine deep **underground,** and then attacking the base of a castle wall or tower. At Rochester Castle they started their tunnel a good distance from the castle. When they were underneath the walls, they dug out a large area and held the roof up with wooden props. Then they filled this space with firewood and set it alight. While the miners retreated, the fire burned through the wood, the roof fell in and the castle wall above caved in. The problem was that those inside the castle simply retreated into the keep and it was necessary to start mining all over again. To ensure that the fire was effective, chunks of lard were used as incendiaries. When attacking Rochester in 1216, King John sent an urgent message to London:

We command you that with all haste by day and night, you send to us 40 bacon pigs of the fattest and those less good for eating to bring fire under the tower.

Other Aids to Attack

Ladders known as **escalades** were used to scale the walls. Having scaled the walls, the attackers used **small artillery** to hurl rocks, stones and burning material at those within the castle. Ladders with movable parts with extending sections (like a fireman's ladder) were also used. A **siege engine**, known as a cat or stork and sometimes mounted on wheels was used by archers.

There were a number of devices to protect attacking forces. These included **mantlets,** transportable screens from which archers and cross bowmen could fire at the enemy and not be hit themselves. Individuals also protected themselves by covering themselves with a wicker, a **wicker siege basket.** Sappers who were responsible for weakening and destroying the walls also had a number of protective devices. For example, the **sapper's cat** or vine was protected by wood covered by hides, turf or even dung. This was winched along. The **sapper's 'mouse'** was used in the same way as a mantlet to enable attackers to get near the wall they intended to sap. It was then turned round so that sappers could work in the safety of its cover.

DEFENCE

As castles developed, the following were important as far as defence was concerned.

1. The **position** of the castle. If it was built on a hill it was easier to defend. If it had natural advantages (like a sheer cliff on one side as at Corfe or the sea on one side as at Caernarfon, Pembroke and Beaumaris) it was again easier to defend.

2. The ease of **taking the battle to the enemy.** In many cases sallies were made on the attackers. Those inside the castle went out, attacked the enemy, especially at night, and then retreated to safety within the castle walls.

3. Using **offensive weapons as defensive ones** such as the catapult, mangonel, trebuchet, scorpion, ballista, great pivoting crossbow, longbow and crossbow.

4. Ensuring there was an adequate supply of **defensive materials** - sand, stones, rotting meat, boiling liquids . . . to tip on invaders from the battlements.

5. Sophistication in **building design** - fewer keeps were constructed. Where they existed there was emphasis on round towers and narrow winding passages to hamper attackers. The development of **concentric design** made castles more difficult to attack and once inside, invaders were trapped between two or more sets of walls.

6. **Spiral Staircases** These wound around a central pillar inside the towers. The staircases gave retreating forces protection and enabled them to fire on pursuers climbing up behind them. The staircases also connected separate storeys of a castle.

7. Sophistication in **detection devices.** People in the castle had to be aware of the presence of sappers and miners so that they could defend themselves against them and not be taken by surprise.

8. **Outworks with Mounds, Ditches and Narrow Entrances** Mounds and ditches built a little way from the castle prevented siege engines being used in an attack. Making the route to a castle narrower slowed down the enemy and made them more vulnerable to attack.

9. **Counter-Mines** If an attempt was made to tunnel under the defences of a castle and emerge within the castle walls, a counter-mine dug above that of the invader allowed the lower mine to be flooded.

Improvements in building methods were very important and Henry II (1154 - 89), King John (1199 - 1216) and Henry III (1216 - 1272) spent large sums of money to improve the defences of their royal castles with the aim of making them impossible to capture.

PRISONS AND TORTURE

Few early castles had special prisons. Prisoners were held below the keep or where goods were stored. Later, prisons were designed as such but they were mainly for hostages held for ransom who were well treated.

Conditions for ordinary prisoners were brutal. Thrown into a damp, dark room, left without food or water, often manacled by their hands and feet, they lay helpless until they starved to death. In the early Middle Ages there was little torture but there was trial by battle or ordeal. Torture was developed both by the state and the Church. The Inquisition in Spain was concerned with saving the souls of heretics and many of these tortures were adopted in Britain.

Methods of torture included putting a prisoner under a board and adding weights on top of it until he confessed to his 'crimes', using red hot pokers to burn a man's skin, remove his eyes or sear other parts of his anatomy. Branding prisoners with a specially designed branding iron also became fashionable. Some prisoners had to endure iron collars and others were fitted with iron masks. The scold's bridle was intended to be used mainly on women. Placed over the victim's head like a cage, it had a piece of metal which fitted into the woman's mouth to stop her from talking. Thumbscrews squashed the thumbs and fingers and later there was the rack: this was designed to stretch the body slowly, a little more each day so that the body was filled with pain.

HAUNTED CASTLES Many people were mistreated or starved to death in castles and it is little wonder that there are many stories of such places being haunted. Few ghosts have been seen but many claim that strange noises can be heard in castles: knocking, the clanking of chains, phantom music or the howl of a dog.

CASTLE BUILDING

We are fortunate in having detailed records about the building of castles in the Middle Ages. Edward I's castles, for example, were financed entirely by the crown and details of the work and expenditure involved are still preserved in the documents at the Public Record Office. These have been the subject of careful research over recent times so that we now know the names of those who worked on the castles, how much they were paid besides the details of the construction and where the materials came from.

The person in charge of building a castle was the master mason. (Today, he would be called an architect.) He designed the building, organised the work and monitored the payment of hundreds of masons, carpenters, craftsmen and builders. He had to be able to keep accounts and write in French and Latin. Master masons were well paid and expected free, comfortable accommodation to be provided.

The master mason began by making sketches of the castle to be built. Then he instructed carpenters to build the site buidings consisting of large wooden shelters (lodges) and, very important, the tracing house. The floor of the tracing house was covered with a layer of hard plaster imported from France. On this plaster the master mason drew the outlines of walls, towers and gateways of the castle to be built. He then gave the free masons the measurements they needed to start work. The masons had to cut ashlar before work could begin - that is cut, then sort and smooth the stone which would be used for the outsides of the walls.

The master carpenter was also important in the building operations. He decided what trees were to be used and those under him made scaffolds, arch supports and wheels to lift the heavy materials needed.

In the Middle Ages, building was a seasonal business carried on between April and November. In the winter months between November and the following April all building ceased and unfinished walls would often be protected from frosts by covering them with straw or thatch. Eight major castles in Wales - Harlech, Builth, Aberystwyth, Flint, Rhuddlan and Conwy - were all completed in about five to seven building seasons.

Building materials were sometimes not available locally and their transport to the castle site had to be carefully planned. Master James of St. George who built many of the Welsh castles had to make sure that money for materials and for paying his men was readily available. This cash came overland from London or York or by sea from Ireland. The money was made up of silver pennies, the only unit of coinage, and it was transported to the building site in wooden barrels.

Raw materials came from as near the castle site as possible. Timber, which was needed in huge quantities, could often be cut from a nearby wood or forest. When this was not possible, it was transported by ship. Wood was needed for initial site stockades, for the wooden lodges, for scaffolding, floors and roofs and for timber framed buildings. Other materials such as stone, lime and sand were again taken from as near the castle as possible but more than one quarry was needed for the enormous quantities required. Whilst glass was seldom used, much of it came from Chester, whilst iron, steel and tin (including nails, cramps, cables and workmen's tools) came from Newcastle-under-Lyme, a centre for the metalworking industry in the Middle Ages.

The first task was to lay the foundations. Labourers were employed to dig, often 10 metres deep. Under stone walls they made a metre deep trench and filled this first with rough rubble. The masons would then use the ashlar they had already cut and prepared for the outside of the walls. The middle of the walls was filled with rough rubble. When the walls were too high to work on from the ground, the masons and carpenters worked on them together using windlasses or treadwheels to lift the heavy stone.

When October arrived the outside work stopped completely. The masons and labourers were laid off until the following April but some of the free masons and carpenters continued to work in the lodges cutting stones and shaping roof beams for the time when work could resume.

In Wales, the Savoy influence may be seen in some of the castles built. P H Humphries points out the following features which are similar in the castles of Savoy and the Edwardian fortresses in Wales:

details such as the frequent use of helicoidal (spiralled) scaffolding in building round towers (indicated by corresponding holes in the masonry); the common occurrence of the Norman style half-round arch; the positioning at Harlech and Rhuddlan, of latrine shafts as shallow butress-like projections at the junction of tower and inner curtain wall; the decoration, at Conwy, of the battlements with triple stone pinnacles; the distinctive window design in the principal rooms at Harlech; and a diagonal inner angle where a corner tower joins the inner curtain walls. These six features rarely occur elsewhere in the British Isles.

P H Humphries, Castles of Edward I in Wales. HMSO 1983 p 12

CASTLES
AND THE NATIONAL CURRICULUM

The study of castles is important for KS3 but it can be included in the curriculum for KS1 in dealing with the lifestyles of people beyond living memory or in KS2 as a local study or in a consideration of domestic and family life in the past.

VISITING HISTORICAL SITES
THE IMPORTANCE OF VISITS

A visit to a castle is useful because it brings the threads of the study together. 'Chalk and talk' are now turned into reality. Pupils can see for themselves the places where people lived and 'seeing is believing'. Observation is the keynote but there may be possibilities of participation in the castle way of life and role play. Fortunately, there are hundreds of castles throughout Britain. Try to visit the selected castle alone before taking a group or class.

PREPARATION FOR A VISIT TO A CASTLE
BEFORE THE VISIT

Choose a castle that is appropriate and can be easily reached or preferably is near to the school. Make a list of the reasons for and the aims of the visit. Decide which National Curriculum topics are to be covered and which attainment targets you wish to meet. If possible visit the castle yourself before you take the class. Most castles have teachers' notes and worksheets which are helpful and save a great deal of time. You may wish to modify them to suit your class and your own objectives. It is very important to prepare the children for the visit. The castle will seem exciting and strange to them when they arrive. They may wander off aimlessly, waste time and possibly get into dangerous situations.

Decide what you are going to tell the children about the castle before the visit. Few are likely to be born archaeologists or natural historians and they need enough information to enable them to understand what they will see during the visit. Slides, photographs, gound/site plans are helpful beforehand if they are available.

You should talk about castles in general before you discuss the one you are planning to visit. It is also a good idea to introduce your pupils to the technical terms of castles (from French and Latin) such as merlons, machicolations, crenellations, donjons (keeps).

One visit is not going to cover everything and so decide exactly what you want to concentrate on. Depending on the ages and abilities of the children, keep it short and keep it simple. Above all, they should enjoy it educationally and socially.

It may be necessary to enhance the children's visual skills. The visit may involve using the following skills at some level.

1. Observation skills.
2. Recording skills.
3. Being able to make comparisons.
4. Being able to make deductions.
5. Reading, writing and comprehension skills.
6. Measuring skills.
7. Estimating skills.
8. The ability to read maps.
9. The ability to read plans.
10. Mathematical skills.
11. Scientific skills.
12. Social skills, especially sharing and communicating.

A sense of time may be learned from the site and youngsters may realise the importance of historical evidence. Aesthetically, the group may gain a great deal from what they see. Pupils need guidance about the information and data they can gather at the castle. The pupils have to relate evidence to function and it is helpful to give them exercises in this before the visit. Also, emphasize the importance of attack and defence. You can consider the class, school, village or town as being under attack. Discuss the weak and strong points of attacking and defending these places before going to the castle.

It is a good idea to make a chart of where you are going to start when you have reached the castle. Draw an exploratory trail on a map and mark the features you want the children to look out for. A time-line of the dates of the building and important events associated with the castle is helpful.

Devise your own activity pack for use on the site. This should include illustrations, a questionnaire and questions requiring observation and deduction. Some children may like to make their own scrapbook about the visit in addition to the work you set them.

TEACHERS' CHECKLIST

AT THE SITE

Make use of the surroundings as well as the buildings. Encourage the children to study the flora, fauna, trees, animal habitats and so on. The children may be able to consider a problem from the past. Examples are:

> You are in charge of providing food and provisions for the castle. How would you go about this task?
> The castle is in danger of attack. What preparations would you make to defend it?
> Show how the castle would have operated (a) in peacetime or (b) in wartime.

Encourage the children to

Make their own Castle Plans

First, draw a diagram of the layout of the castle. Often there is a guide book to help with this. Once the basic plan is drawn, they should mark the positions of such features as the outer walls, keep or great tower, gatehouse, barbican, moat, portcullis and drawbridge.

It is likely that the castle is in ruins so let them look for signs that show where previous structures were. Let them walk through the castle and imagine the many people who once lived there.

History of the Castle

They should find out when and why the castle was built. Have there been other castles on the same site? Have any famous people been associated with it? Who owned the castle in the past and who owns it today? Who looks after it today? Has it been associated with any important events such as battles or sieges?

Checklist for Student Activities at the Castle/Site

1. Look at the location of the castle. Is it on a hill or a slope? Is it built on a river bank or on the coast? Is it located on a rock? Has it got easy access to the sea or water? (e.g., Tower of London and Corfe Castle.)

2. Consider the outside of the castle from the point of view of defence. How good would the defences have been?

3. Look for signs of a moat which may have disappeared. (Sometimes these have been filled in or grassed or used as car parks.) Was the moat fed by a stream? If so consider whether the stream could have been diverted easily. What was the significance of this?

4. Look for the keep. If there is a keep, look for fireplaces: these indicate the number of floors. Holes in walls show where the joists for the floors were. Look for the remains of a spiral staircase in a turret. Look for rooms used as stores, bedrooms, studies or kitchen.

5. Look for the curtain wall/s and note the thickness. Look for any gaps in the battlements, the crenels and the parts of the wall, the merlons, designed to give shelter to those defending the castle. **If it is safe to do so,** walk on the battlements. (Remember children do not always realise how dangerous this can be.)

6. Consider the entrance to the castle. Look for the barbican and the gatehouse. Look for machicolations, holes in the ceiling enabling invaders to be attacked from above. Look for meurtrières or murder holes, holes in the walls through which pikes could be thrust.

7. Do you think there was a portcullis? Grooves in the barbican or gatehouse walls will show where this was.

8. Was there a drawbridge? If so the walls in the gatehouse will have large holes where the ropes or chains used to be.

9. Fireplaces and holes high up in the walls show where floors and rooms used to be.

10. Holes in the walls may show where there used to be beams that held up ceilings.

11. The shape of some rooms will be easy to tell from what is left.

12. In towers and turrets, you should see the remains of spiral staircases leading to rooms above.

13. Lines of stones against inside walls will show the position of buildings inside the castle.

14. Holes in floors might have other explanations e.g. in a courtyard, a hole may indicate a well. Adjacent to a room, a hole may have been a garderobe (a toilet).

15. The size of a room can often be guessed. The Great Hall (the main place for a banquet and gatherings) will be the biggest. The windows, or spaces where they were, will be big and there will be fireplaces against the curtain wall.

16. The place where food was prepared may be discoloured. Look for evidence of a huge fireplace big enough to roast a whole deer. Also there may be a sink, drains, or hooks and spits on which meat and pots were hung for cooking.

17. If there is a basement, look for evidence that prisoners were held there. Some castles still have rings of iron on the wall showing where prisoners were manacled.

18. Look through arrow slits and imagine how archers took aim. Are there any larger holes beneath these arrow slits? If so these are probably cannon holes.

19. Examine the thickness of the walls. It must have taken a lot of effort to collect the stones needed and build such walls. If possible look for debris which may have been used to fill the insides of the walls. This may give a clue to the age of the castle because this practice was discontinued in the 14th. century.

20. Consider the advantages and disadvantages of living in the castles you have visited.

21. Consider the strengths and weaknesses of the castle when it was under attack. How would you defend the castle from attack?

FOLLOW UP TO A VISIT

To reinforce the visit you might consider the following when you return to the classroom.
1. Devise a quiz to find out how much the children have learned.
2. Devise other written work especially making them see the castle as a place where people lived and worked. How did the castle operate on a daily basis? Use actual characters from history if possible.
3. Guide the children to write reports on particular aspects of the castle, the entrance, the keep.
4. Use the activity pack/worksheets/guide book.
5. Organise the pupils to make a display of any written work - drawings, maps, ground plans, photographs ... Develop this for use in the classroom and classify and label any objects. Some children may make models (some accuraely scaled) costumed figures and measured drawings.
6. Pinpoint any technology from the castle.
7. Pinpoint the diet and ways in which food was cooked.
8. Pupils could make a frieze or collage. Brass or other rubbings may be possible.
9. The pupils could write and act a play or situation which might have occurred at the castle such as a conversation between someone who lived in the castle and one of the men-at-arms.
10. Use slides, drawings, photographs and so on to prepare an audio-visual presentation such as tape-slide sequences or video depending on the castle and the age and abilities of the children.
11. Pupils may examine a document - several if available (i.e. copies) from the castle. They could ask themselves

When was it written?   How do we know when it was written?
Who wrote it?   Why was it written?
What sort of document is it? (Personal communication, order or command, official or unofficial . . .)
Are there any differences between this document and others? Compare and contrast the documents if more than one is available.
Is it one of a series of documents?   How do we know the original is genuine?

Finally, it is necessary to evaluate the visit objectively and write a brief report on how such a visit may be improved next time.

SOME CASTLES TO VISIT
ENGLAND

Cumbria
Carlisle
Naworth at Brampton
Derbyshire
Bolsover
Durham
Auckland
Barnard
Durham
Raby
Essex
Hadleigh
Hedingham
Gloucestershire
Berkeley
Sudley
Hertfordshire
Hertford
Kent
Deal
Dover
Hever
Leeds
Lympne
Rochester
Saltwood
Tonbridge
Upnor

Lancashire
Lancaster
Leicestershire
Belvoir
Oakham
Lincolnshire
Bolingbroke
Grinsthorpe
Lincoln
Tattershall
London area
Tower of London
Hampton Court
Windsor
Northamptonshire
Rockingham
Northumberland
Alnwick
Bamburgh
Lindisfarne
Shropshire
Acton Burnell
Bridgnorth
Shrewsbury
Stokesay

Staffordshire
Stafford
Tamworth
East Sussex
Hastings
West Sussex
Arundel
Tyne and Wear
The 'New Castle' at Newcastle
upon Tyne
Warwickshire
Warwick
Kenilworth
West Midlands
Weoley
Dudley
North Yorkshire
Ripley
Scarborough
Skipton

THE WEST COUNTRY

Cornwall
Launceston
Pendennis
Restormel
St Michael's Mount
Tintagel

Devon
Berry Pomeroy
Bickleigh
Lydford
Powderham
Tiverton
Totnes

Dorset
Sherborne Old Castle
Sherborne Castle
Corfe
Portland
Wiltshire
Old Wardour
Lugershall
Wardour New Castle

SCOTLAND

Borders
Ayton, Eyemouth
Floors, Kelso
Hermitage, Liddlesdale
Neidpath, Peebles
Thirlstane, Lauder

Central
Castle Campbell, Dollar
Stirling

Dumfries and Galloway
Caerlaverock, near Thornhill

Fife
Aberdour
Earlshall, near St. Andrews
Kellie, near Pitterweem
St Andrews

Grampians
Balmoral, near Ballater
Braemar
Drum, near Aberdeen
Fyne, near Aberdeen
Kildaunray, Donside

Highlands
Brodie, near Nairn
Cawdor, near Inverness
Dunrobin, Golspie
Dunvegan, Isle of Skye
Eilean Donar, West Ross

Lothian
Dirleton
Edinburgh
Lufness, Aberlady
Tantallon, North Berwick

Strathclyde
Inverary, Argyll
Penkill, Girvan
Newark, Port Glasgow
Brodick, Isle of Arran

Tayside
Blair, Blair Atholl
Castle Menzies, Weem
Elcho,
Glamis
Kellie, Arbroath

WALES

Clwyd
Chirk
Denbigh
Ewloe
Flint
Hawarden
Rhuddlan
Ruthin

Dyfed
Aberystwyth
Carew
Carreg Cennen
Cilgerran
Kidwelly
Llanstephan
Manorbier
Pembroke
Picton

Mid Glamorgan
Caerphilly
Coity
Ogmore

South Glamorgan
Cardiff
Castell Coch

West Glamorgan
Oystermouth
Weobley

Powys
Bronllys
Painscastle
Powis
Tretower

Gwent
Abergavenny
Caldicot
Chepstow
Grosmont
Penhow
Raglan
Skenfrith
Whitecastle

Gwynedd
Beaumaris
Caernarfon
Castell-y-Bere
Conwy (Conway)
Criccieth
Dolbadarn

A NOTE ON PROJECT WORK

A list of projects on castles appears at the end of the pupils' worksheets. These may be used with individuals or with a group of students to prepare an expanded piece of writing on the subject. Collaboration in work is important and each child may be given a special part of the project to study. Consideration of a local castle is a good beginning: there is likely to be easy access to written records and the children can see the site for themselves. Such a study would fulfil National Curriculum requirements for local history work. Suppose the class was within easy reach of Corfe Castle and chose this as a basis for their project work. The themes they could study include:

The history of the castle.
Corfe Castle compared with others in the West Country.
Position/location of the castle.
Castle architecture/the castle's defences.
Life in Corfe Castle.
Famous people connected with Corfe Castle.
Corfe Castle in peace.
Corfe Castle in war.
Life in Corfe Castle in the Middle Ages.
Corfe Castle and the town.
Corfe Castle today.
Developments/changes concerning the castle.
Corfe Castle and the English Civil War.

This list is not exhaustive by any means. Sketches, drawings and models make the work more interesting. Some students may prefer to take photographs. The combined results can then be combined into a file.

In any event, decide on the main topic first and make sure the children understand any difficult or new terms they may come across. They may need to consult a dictionary at this initial stage and a combined vocabulary list obtained. Some key words are

armour	drawbridge	mangonel	portcullis
armourer	dungeon	marshall	reeve
arrow slit	gatehouse	medieval	retinue
beam holes	gun loop	merlon	sapping
bailey	household	mining	seneschal
barbican	inner ward	moat	site
baron	keep	motte	spiral staircase
battering ram	king	murder holes	square keep
battlement	knight	noble	tower
concentric castle	lady-in-waiting	Norman	trebuchet
crossbow	location	outer ward	wall walks
curtain wall	machicolations		

A topic web and discussion/guidance as to how information can be obtained should get the students started. Check the key words and the topic web themes against the subject index in the local library. The children can then consult them as they proceed. Then check for any other sources of information. The castle itself would be an obvious place to start - guide books, activity packs, postcards and so on. There may be places to write to for information. The children can look for posters, photographs, local magazines or film strips. Encourage the children to make careful notes on the most important facts as they discover them and to keep details about their sources of information. Finally, they can draft their work and revise it until you and they are satisfied with it. It is important to check project work as it proceeds and to be sure that each child is up to date.

USEFUL ADDRESSES

Archaeology in Education
Department of Archaeology and Prehistory
University of Sheffield
Sheffield S10 2TN
Tel 01742 768555 ext 6081

The Archaeological Resource Centre
St Saviour Gate
York YO1 2NN
Tel 01904 654 32

Area Museum Council for the South West
Hestercombe House
Cheddon Fitzpaine
Taunton
Somerset TA2 8LQ
Tel 01823 259696

Arts Council of Great Britain
14 Great Peter Street
London SwIP 3NQ
Tel 0171 333 0100

Cadw Welsh Historic Monuments
9th Floor
Brunel House
2 Fitzalan Road
Cardiff CF2 1UY
Tel 01222 465511

Central Bureau for Educational Visits
    and Exchanges
Seymour Mews House
Seymour Mews
London WIH 9PE
Tel 0171 486 5101

The Civic Trust
Education Department
17 Carlton House Terrace
London SW1Y 5AW
Tel 0171 930 0914

Countryside Commission
John Dower House
Crescent Place
Cheltenham
Glos GL50 3RA
Tel 01242 521381

Countryside Council for Wales
Plas Penrhos
Fford Penrhos
Bangor
Gwynedd LL57 2LQ
Tel 01248 370444

English Heritage
Education Service
Keysign House
429 Oxford Street
London S1R 2HT
Tel 0171 973 3000

Field Studies Council
Preston Montford
Montford Bridge
Shrewsbury
Shropshire SY4 1HW
Tel 01743 850674

The Geographical Association
343 Fulwood Road
Sheffield S10 3BP
Tel 01742 670666

Group for Education in Museums
63 Navarino Road
London E8 1AG
Tel 0171 249 4296

Historical Association
59A Kennington Park Road
London SE11 4JH
Tel 0171 735 3901

Ironbridge Institute
The Ironbridge Gorge Museum
Ironbridge
Telford
Shropshire TF8 7AW
Tel 01952 432751

London Tourist Board
26 Grosvenor Gardens
London SW1W 0DU
Tel 0171 730 3450

Museums Association
42 Clerkenwell Close
London EC1R 0PA
Tel 0171 608 2933

National Association for
    Environmental Education
University of Wolverhampton
Walsall Campus
Gorway
Walsall WS1 3BD
Tel 01922 31200

National AudioVisual Aids Library
The Arts Building
Normal College
Siliwen Road
Bangor
Gwynedd LL57 2D
Tel 01248 370144

National Farmers' Union
Information Division
22 Longacre
London WC2E 9LY
Tel 0171 331 7200

National Trust
Educational Manager
36 Queen Anne's Gate
London SW1H 9AS
Tel 0171 222 9251

National Trust for Scotland
Education Officer
5 Charlotte Square
Edinburgh EH2 4DU
Tel 0131 226 5922

Young Archaeologists Club
The Council for British Archaeology
Bowes Morrell House
111 Walmgate
York YO1 2VA
Tel 01904 671417

Wales Tourist Board
Brunel House
2 Fitzalan Road
Cardiff CF2 1UY
Tel 01222 499909

PUPILS' RESOURCES - WORKSHEETS

A CASTLE

1. What kind of castle is in the drawing above?

2. What were these castles made of?

3. Where did the nobleman reside in this type of castle?

4. How difficult was it to defend a castle like this?

5. Were these castles built in   A the 10th century   B the 11th century
                                     C the 12th century   D later than this?

6. What type of castle was built later?

EARLY CASTLES

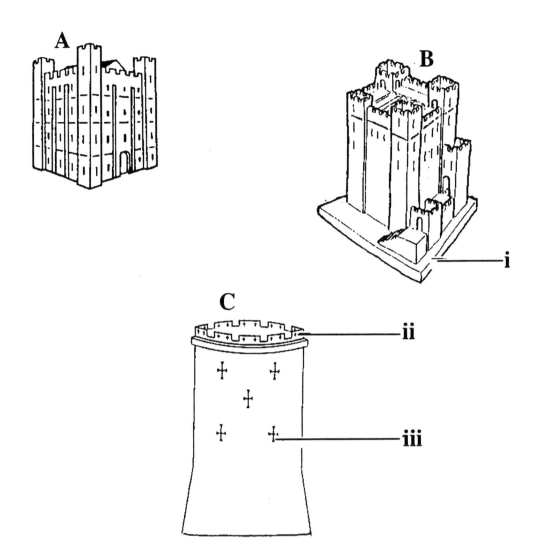

1. What kinds of castles are A B and C?

2. What were these castles made of? How do they differ from earlier castles?

3. Which is the most developed of these castles? Which is the earliest and which is the latest structure?

4. Name the features marked   B i   C ii   C iii.

5. Which of the castles A, B and C was most easily defended? Give a reason for your answer.

6. Imagine you are the constable of one of these early castles. Outline your responsibilities and duties.

INSIDE A KEEP

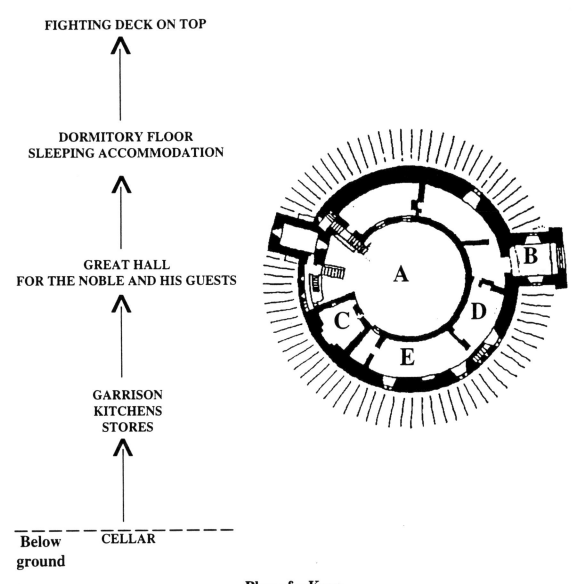

FIGHTING DECK ON TOP

↑

DORMITORY FLOOR
SLEEPING ACCOMMODATION

↑

GREAT HALL
FOR THE NOBLE AND HIS GUESTS

↑

GARRISON
KITCHENS
STORES

↑

**Below
ground**   **CELLAR**

Plan of a Keep

1. The diagrams above show the structure of a stone keep. People climbed from storey to storey by ladders or spiral staircases. Why were the staircases spiral?

2. Name the structures A, B, C, D, E. What was the area shaded ⬚ ?

3. Fighting took place from the top of the keep but the garrison was accommodated at ground level. Why was this a disadvantage?

4. The keep has been called the 'nerve-centre of a castle'. What do you think this means? Do you think it is an accurate description? Give reasons for your answer.

5. Outline the activities that took place on each level of a keep.

6. Write an account of the advantages and disadvantages of the stone keep.

A TWELFTH CENTURY CASTLE

1. Mark the following features on the castle above

1. The keep
2. Outer bailey
3. The curtain walls (2 sets)
4. The gatehouse
5. The moat

6. Three round towers
7. A merlon
8. A crenel
9. An arrow loop
10. A wall walk

2. Describe the castle in your own words.

3. If you lived in this castle, who would you like to be? Give reasons for your answer.

A BARBICAN AND GATEHOUSE

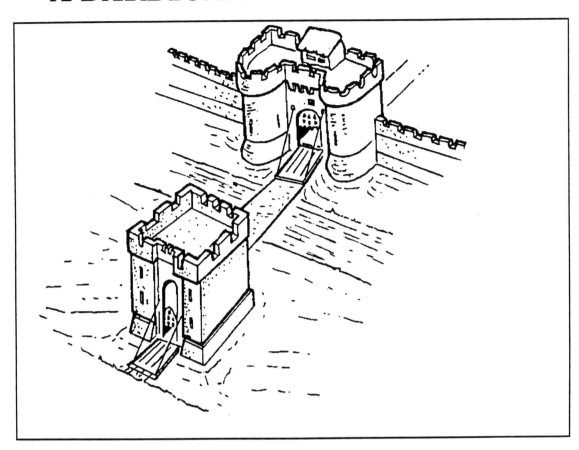

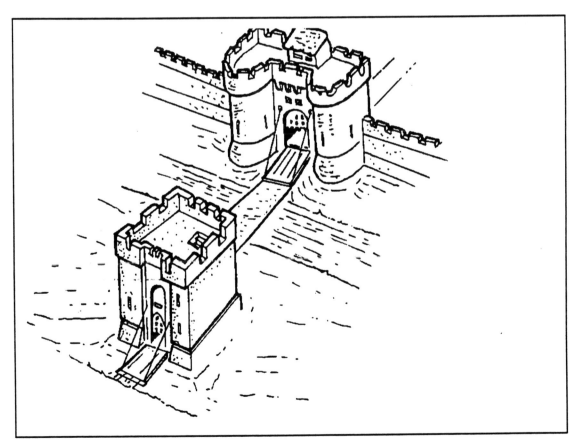

These are two pictures of a barbican and gatehouse. Find ten differences between the two pictures. Outline how you would attack such a well defended stronghold.

DEFENSIVE STRUCTURES

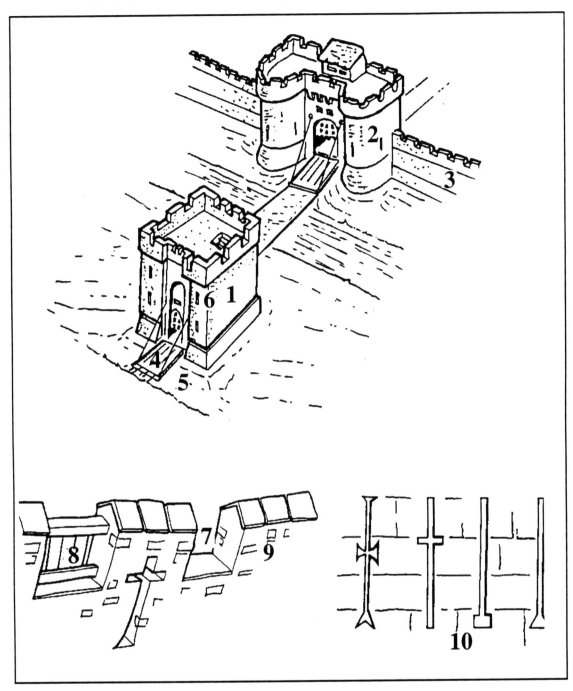

These drawings show some of the defensive structures in a concentric castle.
Name them.

1. ———————————   6. ———————————

2. ———————————   7. ———————————

3. ———————————   8. ———————————

4. ———————————   9. ———————————

5. ———————————   10. ———————————

A KNIGHT

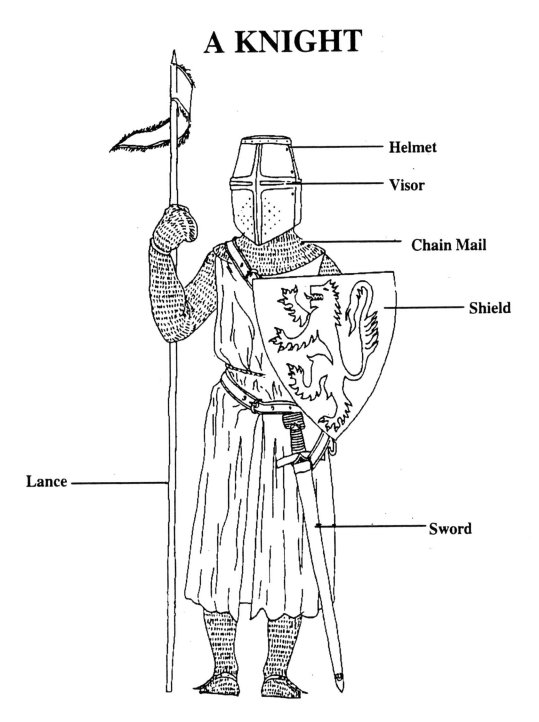

Helmet

Visor

Chain Mail

Shield

Lance

Sword

Study this picture of a knight then answer the questions below.

1. Who were knights?

2. How did a man become a knight?

3. The shield is really the knight's coat of arms. What do you understand by a 'coat of arms'?

4. Why was it necessary for knights to have coats of arms?

5. This is an early knight. How can you tell this? What happened to knights' armour by the end of the 14th. century?

6. Explain what is meant by (a) a tournament, (b) a mêlée, and (c) a joust.

7. Write a page on the training and life of a knight in the early 14th. century. Why was this considered to be an honourable profession for young men?

DESIGN A COAT OF ARMS

In the 12th. century, knights began to wear helmets and armour that covered their bodies and hid their faces completely. It was impossible to tell whether a knight was friend or foe. They put crests on their helmets and distinctive designs (often called cognisances or devices) on their shields, on their lance pennons and on their surcoats so that they could be recognised. (Surcoats were loose robes worn over their armour and called coats of arms. Some were richly embroidered like the surcoat of the Black Prince: a replica hangs above his tomb in Canterbury Cathedral.) Ladies could not wear arms in this way and they put them on a diamond shape, called a lozenge, for example, the arms borne by the Queen when when she was Princess Elizabeth.

The colours used in heraldry are blue, red, green, purple and black as well as gold and silver. Study the design on your school shield. What is its significance?

Below is a drawing of the coat of arms of the Marshall family, Earls of Pembroke. The same arms became the emblem of the Bigod family, the Earls of Norfolk. The Marshalls and the Bigods had control over Chepstow Castle for most of the 13th. and 14th. centuries. Why do you think it has a dragon?

Design a coat of arms for your family or your school. Use colours and designs that you think say something about them. For example, if sport is important, you might use objects associated with this.

A lion rampant

An eagle displayed

A fleur-de-lis

A cross engrailed

Colour this coat of arms of the Marshall family.
The background on the left is yellow.
The background on the right is green.
The dragon is red.

A cross flory

Some of the symbols used in coats of arms on shields.

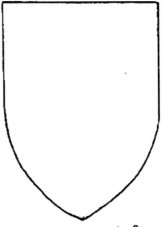

Design and draw your own coat of arms.

JOUSTING

Study the picture above and describe in your own words, 'Jousting in Medieval Times'. Explain why jousting was so popular.

A CASTLE PLAN

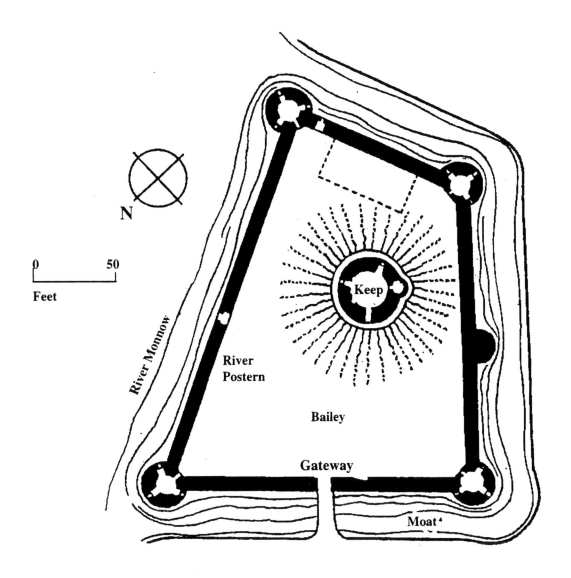

PLAN OF SKENFRITH CASTLE

Study this plan of Skenfrith Castle.

1. What can you learn about the castle from this plan?

2. Draw a plan of a castle you know or have visited.

3. Compare your plan with that of Skenfrith Castle and describe any differences between the two castles.

A CASTLE UNDER ATTACK

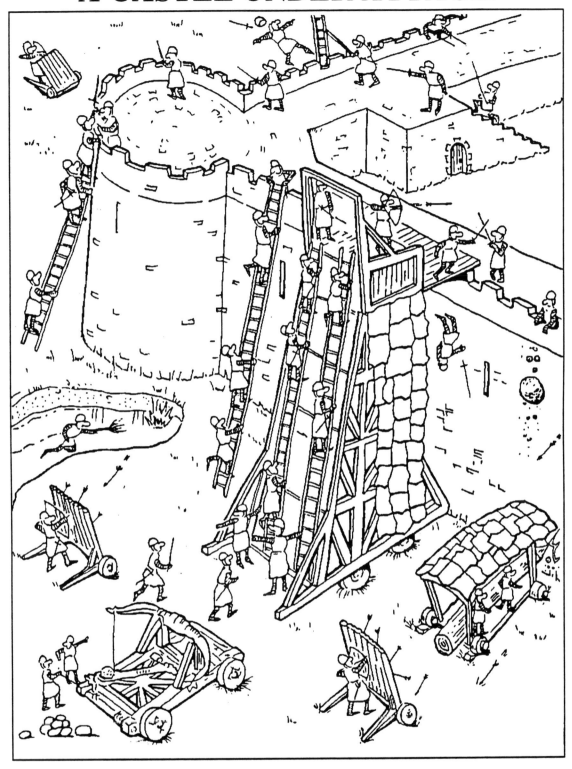

1. This humorous picture of a castle under attack tells us a great deal about warfare in medieval times. Give an account of the methods of attack you have learned about. Illustrate your answer with diagrams.

2. Explain either how (a) a belfry or (b) a battering ram worked.

3. Two siege methods (the use of a trebuchet and sapping) are omitted from this picture. Why do you think they were not used here?

4. Explain why the drawing is humorous?

DEFENDING A CASTLE

Complete the story below. Your ending may be happy or sad.

It is the silence, the strange quiet, which is the most disturbing. We were all asleep when the attack first came. The noise sent us scurrying about in panic. Then there was the smell of burning and . . .

PRISONERS AND TORTURE

1. What can you learn about conditions and torture in the castles of medieval times from this humorous drawing of the inside of a dungeon?

2. In the picture, there at least five ways in which people were tortured. Name them.

3. Why is the picture humorous?

4. Complete the story below in your own words.
   Sir Lancelot knew others were there imprisoned with him. There were sighs, soft moans and strange stirrings in the darkness. A spider crawled along his bare arm and he felt a long, hairy body scramble over his right leg. Suddenly . . .

A CASTLE FEAST

1. Describe the scene in you own words. Where and when do you think the meal is taking place? Who is sitting on the main table? Where do the others sit? Who organises the food for such a meal?

2. 'After the meal was finished, the baron called for some entertainment. Musicians and jugglers appeared as if from nowhere. After half-an-hour of these amusements ...' Complete this account of a visit to the castle.

FOOD AND COOKING

1. Read this passage and then answer the questions below.

Bread was a very important part of the diet. Its quality varied depending on the grain and how it was ground. It was supposed to be taken to the manorial mill but was often illicitly ground on a hand quern at home and the flour obtained was gritty. The most important use of brown bread for the wealthy was as trenchers or plates. These were made by cutting stale bread into thick slices with a slight hollow in the centre. A nobleman would use several trenchers at each meal. Afterwards they were given to the poor. An ordinary person would have one trencher per meal, possibly shared between two people. Bread was expensive and most people baked their own. Servants and serfs complained that they only had coarse brown bread while the wealthy kept the white for themselves and considered it to be a status symbol.

1. Why did the quality of bread vary?
2. Why was flour made using a hand quern gritty?
3. What was a trencher?
4. Why were the poor glad to receive the used trenchers from the table of a nobleman?
5. What kind of bread did servants have and why did they complain about it?
6. Give the meaning of the following as used in the passage: diet, quality, illicitly, quern, stale, hollow, nobleman, expensive, coarse, status symbol

2. Read this passage and then answer the questions below.

The kitchen of a castle, manor house or monastery was sometimes in a separate building because of the danger of a fire. It was usually made of stone with a stone floor. There would be a large wide fireplace, sometimes two, where most of the food was cooked. Spits big enough to cook a whole pig turned over a fire, dripping fat sizzling and flashing in the heat. Soups and vegetables were cooked in large cauldrons suspended over the fire. Cooking was on a grand scale in the kitchens of prosperous families and the kitchen developed into a maze of rooms: larders, storerooms, cellars, a buttery, pantry, dairy, bakehouse. There were no kitchen maids or female cooks. Scullion boys turned the large spits, cleaned ladles, knives, brushes and bowls, scrubbed the kitchen floor and slept on it at night. The kitchen had to feed everyone in the castle with people eating different food according to their position in the hierarchy of the castle.

A typical menu might consist of:

Squirrel stew or rabbit broth
Trout with apple
Shellfish scented with jasmine and rosemary
Boar's head with brawn
Spiced roast ox
Roast swan - a delicacy in medieval times
Blancmange - a savoury dish in earlier times
Apples, figs, nuts
Cakes with honey
Wine

---

1. Explain the meaning of
'Cooking was on a grand scale'.
'The kitchen . . . was sometimes in a separate building because of the danger of fire.'
' . . . with people eating different food according to their position in the hierarchy of the castle.'

2. Give the meaning of the following as used in the passage: sizzling, flashing, buttery, pantry, hierarchy.

3. Why was food, especially meat, cooked and eaten as soon as possible after the animal had been killed?

4. Suppose you are a scullion boy working in the kitchen of a large castle. Describe the preparations for the visit of an important lord and his retinue.

THE CASTLE TIMES

You are a special correspondent with *The Castle Times,* a leading newspaper.
Remember to illustrate all your reports and stories with drawings, paintings, or cartoons.

1. **As a wartime reporter, you have been asked to give an eyewitness account of the siege of a neighbouring castle.**

[Remember to include the preparations for the siege, the reasons for it, the timing of the siege, the actual siege - noise, smells, fear and excitement, the feelings and emotions of those attacking and defending the castle, the weaponry used, how long the siege lasts and how it ends, the number of injured and dead. The future of the castle.]

2. **Write a letter to your parents or a friend from the besieged castle.**

3. **When the siege is over, you are expected to interview the victor personally.**

[This is an exclusive interview. Personal details are needed including picture (drawing) of the victor, his name, age, where he was born and grew up, family (were his sons in the attacking/defending forces)? Reasons for the siege, his role and reactions to the success. The factors which helped him to succeed. His views on the future of the castle.]

4. **You visit the castle the day after the siege has ended and interview the people who survived.**

[Describe the scene within the castle - noise, smells, colours, atmosphere. Find out how people survived. What did they eat? Were they short of water? How did they treat the sick and wounded? How do they feel about the outcome? Were many children involved? Could the siege have been ended earlier? What are the people doing - repairs, wandering aimlessly? What do they see as their future?]

5. **A year later, the castle is visited by the King and his retinue. You are expected to produce a diary of the preparations for the visit and the daily events in the castle and the surrounding countryside while the monarch is there.**

[Describe the preparations - forward party to liaise with the constable and get the castle ready. All visible signs of the siege of the previous year are removed or repaired. Effect on the people living near the castle. Cleaning of castle, food stored - livestock, hay, grain, drinks. King and party arrive. Daily events - courts, fines, taxes collected, feasts, hunting trips, entertainment. Exclusive interviews with members of the party. Departure of the King. Castle gets back to normal.]

HISTORICAL SOURCES

1. *We command you that with all haste by day and night, you send to us 40 bacon pigs of the fattest and those less good for eating to bring fire under the tower.*

King John, (Rochester)

2. *It was customary for the rich men and nobles of those parts, because their chief occupation is the carrying on of feuds and slaughters, in order that they may in this way be safe from enemies, and may have the greater power for either conquering their equals or keeping down their inferiors, to heap up a mound of earth as high as they were able, and to dig round it a broad, open and deep ditch, and to girdle the whole upper edge of the mound, instead of a wall, with a barrier of wooden planks, stoutly fixed together with numerous turrets set round. Within was constructed a house or rather citadel, commanding the whole, so that the gate of entry could only be approached by a bridge, which, first sprinting from the counterscarp of the ditch, was gradually raised as it advanced, supported by sets of piers, two or even three, trussed on each side over convenient spans, crossing the ditch with a managed ascent so as to reach the upper level of the mound, landing at its edge on a level at the threshold of the gate.*

(12th. century French writer. Translated.)

These are writings from contemporary sources. Answer the following questions on them.

1. 1. Which is the earlier of the writings? Give reasons for your answer.

    2. Why did King John want fat pigs?

    3. Why did King John want to light a fire? Was he cold?

    4. Explain the phrase 'bring fire under the tower'?

    5. The words of King John describe the work of those connected with the destruction of a castle. What were these people called?

    6. What castle was involved in the King's message?

2. 1. What type of castle is being described in the second passage?

    2. Draw an example of the castle being described.

    3. '. . . a house or rather citadel' - what does this mean?

    4. '. . . a barrier of wooden planks' - give one word for this.

EVERYDAY LIFE IN A CASTLE

1. **Imagine you are a young squire and write an account of how you live. You get up at sunrise and this is a list of the tasks you might have to carry out. How does your life as a young squire differ from the way you live today?**

   1. Clear away your mattress from the Great Hall.
   2. Attend mass in the chapel.
   3. Help your master, a knight, to get dressed.
   4. Break your fast.
   5. Learn Latin with a priest.
   6. Learn how to ride a war-horse. Take a turn at the quintain.
   7. Clean your master's armour by rolling it in a barrel of sand.
   8. Attend the table in the Great Hall.
   9. Fall asleep at sunset.

2. **The wife of a farmer or labourer had to work very hard in the fields and at home. In the fields she helped with weeding, planting seeds and harvesting the crops. In the house she made bread, cheese and butter, cooked all the meals, spun and wove cloth, washed and mended clothes. The farmer's wife milked the cows and tended the pigs. It was difficult to keep the home bright and sparkling when it was shared with farm animals such as sheep and oxen. Because so many babies and young children died, families were large. If the children were ill, the wife had to be nurse as well as mother. A farmer's wife had little time for luxuries like learning to read and write.**
   Imagine you are the wife of a farmer in medieval times. Write an account of a day in your life. How does it differ from the way you live today?

3. **Much less is known about the way women lived in medieval times and what they did. Suggest reasons for this.**

4. **Imagine you are a war-horse belonging to a knight. Give an account of one of your engagements with your master.**

5. **If you were asked to build a castle, where would you build it and why?**
   Draw a plan of your castle.

6. **Do you think castles should be preserved? Give reasons for your answer.**

7. **Castle building had virtually stopped by the end of the 16th. century. Why was this?**

8. **'It is unlikely that many modern buildings will survive as well as castles have. Do you agree with this statement? Give reasons for your answer.**

9. **'Large buildings are more difficult to build today than castles were.' Do you agree? Give reasons for your answer.**

10. **If someone from medieval times was 'magically transported' to today's world, what do you think would most surprise him or her? Give reasons for your answer.**

A CASTLE DICTIONARY

Fill in the boxes

MEANING	WORD
1 Dressed stone facing	1
2 Courtyard or ward	2
3 Merlons, embrasures	3
4 Toilets	4
5 Fence of wooden stakes	5
6 Private sitting room	6
7 Place for storing family clothes, money, jewels and silver	7
8 Person in charge of all the manors, market places and courts	8
9 Person in charge of the chapels and priests	9
10 Person who handed out left-over food and cast-off clothes to the poor	10
11 Person in charge of all indoor servants	11
12 Person in charge of all outdoor servants	12
13 Person who paid all the bills and kept accounts	13
14 Young boy who served two knights	14
15 An area where knights practised	15
16 A special horse rode in battles	16
17 A mock battle between two teams of knights	17
18 Public show of knights fighting for entertainment	18
19 Two knights fighting in armed combat	19
20 A loose coat decorated with badges	20
21 An organisation set up to regulate the use of insignia	21

A CASTLE QUIZ

1. What is meant by a castle?

2. Why were castles first built?

3. What was a burgh?

4. What do you understand by a motte?

5. What do you understand by a bailey?

6. What is a motte and bailey castle?

7. What is a keep?

8. What do you understand by the great hall?

9. What is meant by a forebuilding?

10. What is a palisade?

11. Give the name for 'a keep built in the form of a circular wall enclosing the motte top, or even the entire motte, and surrounding the castle's living quarters.'

12. What is a curtain wall?

13. 'Later castles were strengthened by outer or curtain walls, built in rings with the same centre.' What were these castles called?

14. What is (a) a moat and (b) a drawbridge?

15. What is a portcullis?

16. What is the gatehouse of a castle?

17. At first single gatehouses were built. How did this change by the 13th. century?

18. What is the barbican of a castle?

19. What are meurtrières?

20. What were toilets in medieval castles called?

21. What do you understand by
    (a) an oratory
    (b) a piscina
    (c) a solar?

22. 'An overhanging parapet on the outer wall of a castle, often placed over a portcullis, with holes in its floor for dropping sand, stones, boiling liquids and missiles on an enemy.' What is being described?

23. What is a loop in a castle wall?

24. What is the rear exit of a castle called?

25. What was a castle 'squint'?

26. Name the equivalent of an architect in medieval times.

27. Name the famous architect mainly responsible for building Edward I's castles in Wales. What nationality was he?

28. (a) Originally, what was a coat of arms?
    (b) What did a coat of arms come to mean later?

29. Name the main official in a castle after the baron.

30. Who took charge of the accounts in a castle?

A CASTLE FRIEZE

Colour this picture of a knight. Make several like him, cut them out and make a frieze or use other pictures from this book as well to make a collage showing life in medieval times.

Write the missing words in the spaces in the following passage:

In the Middle Ages, boys from noble families often trained to become . . . .   A young boy started his apprenticeship as a   . . . .   Later he became a   . . . . . .
Knights practised their skills in a special area called a   . . . .   The knight rode at a special target, the   . . . .   and tried to hit it with his   . . . . .   The target was weighted so that it swung back and hit any careless or untrained rider. Knights also practised by fighting each other in mock duels. Sometimes these   . . . . . .   were held in front of a crowd for entertainment at a   . . . .   Each knight rode a
. . .   .   and wore chain mail or a suit of   . . . . . .
So that he could be identified, a knight wore a   . . . .   which bore the badges or insignia of his master.

CASTLE MATHS

1. The towers in Conwy Castle are over 21 metres high and 9 metres in diameter. The walls are up to 4.5 metres thick. Use these figures to calculate the approximate volume of stone used to build one of these towers. [$\pi = \frac{22}{7}$]

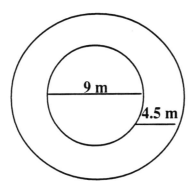

9 m

4.5 m

2. If the average size of the stones to cover the outside face of a tower in question 1 is 20 cm x 30 cm, how many of these stones are needed for one tower? [$\pi = \frac{22}{7}$]

3. Two of Edward I's campaigns to subdue the Welsh cost approximately £23,000 for the first and £80,000 for the second. To obtain the costs today, these figures must be multiplied by 600. What would the campaigns cost today?

4. The passage below is from an inventory of stores and furniture delivered to a castle for the king's use at a religious feast in 1346. It tells us how a castle was provisioned at this time.

'22 quarters of wheat . . . 27 quarters of oats, half a carcass of salt beef . . . 60 carcasses of salted muttons, of which 30 were putrid, 19 small bacons, 8 tuns of Gascony wine, 11 tuns of white wine . . . 8 quarters of coarse salt, 1 rick of hay, estimated at 12 cart loads, 2 empty tuns . . . 1 hanging bell for the chapel, 2 moveable tables . . . 4 pairs of trestles . . . 1 bucket bound with iron for drawing water . . . 2 old hawsers for working the drawbridge . . . 1 great net for catching large animals or wild fowl . . . 6 nets for catching hares, 4 ladders, 1 bier for the sepulchre in the chapel, 2 pairs of fetters . . . 1 iron chain and collar, 2 iron chairs, broken and of scarcely any value . . .'

This is careful accounting 14th. century style. What do these facts, figures and details tell us about life in the Middle Ages?

PUZZLES

1. A message smuggled out of the besieged castle read

DV ZIV YVHRVTVW. KOVZHV HVMW SVOK.

What did it mean?

Code used

A	B	C	D	E	F	G	H	I	J	K	L	M
Z	Y	X	W	V	U	T	S	R	Q	P	O	N

N	O	P	Q	R	S	T	U	V	W	X	Y	Z
M	L	K	J	I	H	G	F	E	D	C	B	A

The reply promised help.

I WILL SEND FIFTY KNIGHTS AT ONCE.

Write the reply in code.

2.   WORDSQUARE

Find the following in the word square:
(Each letter may be used more than once or not at all.)

1. Pulled up in case of attack.
2. Safest part of a castle.
3. Poet.
4. Head of a castle.
5. Castles.
6. Defensive wall.
7. Shot from a bow.
8. Coat - - - - - -.
9. Surrounds a castle and is
   full of water.
10. Aperture for arrows.
11. Battle between knights.

B	R	I	D	G	E	K	Y
A	Y	L	O	R	D	E	C
R	O	O	F	O	C	E	U
D	U	O	F	O	F	P	R
W	D	P	I	M	O	A	T
A	R	R	O	W	R	A	A
L	A	R	M	S	T	D	I
L	W	J	O	U	S	T	N

3. The following may be found in a castle. What are they?

**TTEOM,   EPKE,   LAIYBE,   TRAUCNI LWLA,   OGTEUESAH,
INBRBAAC,   DRMEUR LSOEH,   URLPCLISOT,   OLPO,   TOMA**

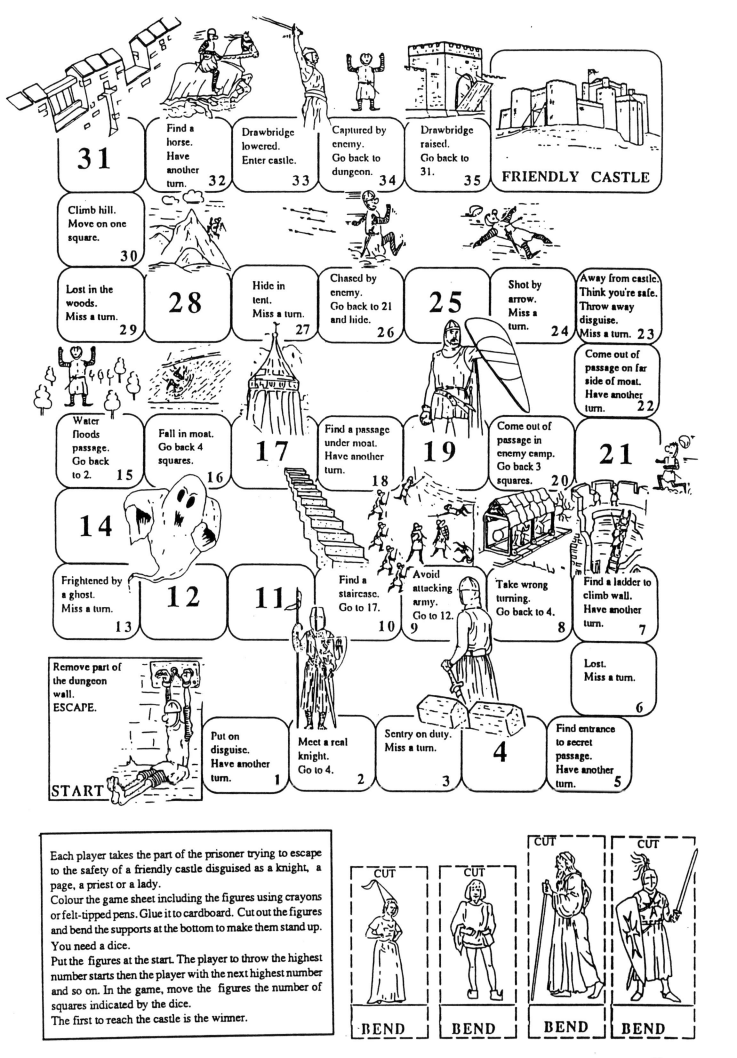

31

Find a horse. Have another turn. **32**

Drawbridge lowered. Enter castle. **33**

Captured by enemy. Go back to dungeon. **34**

Drawbridge raised. Go back to 31. **35**

FRIENDLY CASTLE

Climb hill. Move on one square. **30**

Lost in the woods. Miss a turn. **29**

28

Hide in tent. Miss a turn. **27**

Chased by enemy. Go back to 21 and hide. **26**

25

Shot by arrow. Miss a turn. **24**

Away from castle. Think you're safe. Throw away disguise. Miss a turn. **23**

Come out of passage on far side of moat. Have another turn. **22**

Water floods passage. Go back to 2. **15**

Fall in moat. Go back 4 squares. **16**

17

Find a passage under moat. Have another turn. **18**

19

Come out of passage in enemy camp. Go back 3 squares. **20**

21

14

Frightened by a ghost. Miss a turn. **13**

12

11

Find a staircase. Go to 17. **10**

Avoid attacking army. Go to 12. **9**

Take wrong turning. Go back to 4. **8**

Find a ladder to climb wall. Have another turn. **7**

Lost. Miss a turn. **6**

Remove part of the dungeon wall. ESCAPE.

START

Put on disguise. Have another turn. **1**

Meet a real knight. Go to 4. **2**

Sentry on duty. Miss a turn. **3**

4

Find entrance to secret passage. Have another turn. **5**

Each player takes the part of the prisoner trying to escape to the safety of a friendly castle disguised as a knight, a page, a priest or a lady.

Colour the game sheet including the figures using crayons or felt-tipped pens. Glue it to cardboard. Cut out the figures and bend the supports at the bottom to make them stand up.

You need a dice.

Put the figures at the start. The player to throw the highest number starts then the player with the next highest number and so on. In the game, move the figures the number of squares indicated by the dice.

The first to reach the castle is the winner.

CUT   CUT   CUT   CUT

BEND   BEND   BEND   BEND

PROJECT IDEAS

1. History of the Castles of Britain.
2. History of the Castles of Wales.
3. History of the Castles of the West Country.
4. History of the Castles of Scotland.
5. London's Castles.
6. A Study of a Local Castle.
7. Castle Life.
8. Medieval Castle Sieges.
9. The Art of War in the Middle Ages.
10. Castle Defences.
11. Everyday Life of Medieval Men and Women.
12. A Famous Castle Siege.
13. The King and his Castles.
14. The Castles of Edward 1st.
15. Moats in the Middle Ages.
16. The Role of Men in Castle Society.
17. The Role of Women in Castle Society.
18. Knights, A Study of the Way They Lived and their Role in Castle Society.
19. The Castle at its Zenith.
20. The Reasons for the Decline of Castles.
21. A Study of Castles in the 10th. Century.
22. A Study of Castles in the 11th. Century.
23. A Study of Castles in the 12th. Century.
24. A Study of Castles in the 13th. Century.
25. A Study of Castles in the 14th. Century.
26. A Study of Castles in the 15th. Century.
27. Castles in Tudor Times.
28. Castles and the English Civil War.
29. The Development of Fortified Manor Houses.
30. The Tower of London.
31. Warwick Castle, Warwick.
32. The History and Importance of Caernarfon Castle.
33. Windsor Castle.
34. A Study of Castle Building.
35. Castle Banquets.
36. Castles for the Rich.
37. Fake Castles.
38. The Legacy of the Middle Ages - Castles.
39. Why we should investigate Castles.
40. Castle Ghosts.
41. A Study of Castles that are lived in Today.
42. Castles and the Development of Towns.
43. Pre-Historic Castles.
44. The Preservation of Castles.
45. The work of one of the following with reference to Castles:
    (a) The National Trust.
    (b) The National Trust for Scotland.
    (c) English Heritage.
    (d) Cadw Welsh Historic Monuments.
46. 'Building Castles in the Air.'
47. Castle Menus.
48. Stone Keeps.
49. Norman Castles.
50. Angevin Castles.
51. Plantagenet Castles.
52. Castle Heroes or a Famous Castle Hero.
53. Castle Prisoners and Torture.
54. A Famous Castle Prisoner.
55. Castle Provisions.
56. Norman Towns and Castle Planning.
57. Castles of Enceinte.
58. Master James of St. George.
59. Castles in Brick.
60. A Study of why Man built Castles.
61. Castle Myths.
62. Castle Art.
63. Castle Artifices.
64. Siege Weapons.
65. Weapons of Attack in Castles.
66. Weapons for defending Castles.
67. Armour.
68. The Development of Coats of Arms.
69. English Castles 1050 - 1600.
70. A Visit to a Famous Castle.
71. The Everyday Lives of Boys and Girls in Medieval Castles.
72. Gothic Castles.
73. Sham Castles.
74. The Use of Castles Today.
75. What can be learned from visiting a Castle.
76. A Study of the Importance of the Location of a Named Castle.
77. A Comparison of the Life of a Nobleman with that of a Farmer in the Middle Ages.
78. A Study of the Diet of People who lived in the Middle Ages and how it differed from the Food eaten Today.
79. Cooking in the Middle Ages.
80. Class Divisions in Society in the Middle Ages.

ANSWERS

Pages 29, 30 See teachers' notes.

Suggested structures in the keep, page 31
Chapel, kitchen, courtyard, bed chamber, great hall, guard room, solar . . .

Ten Differences, page 33

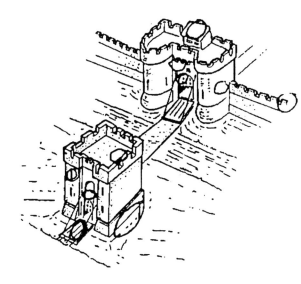

Defensive Structure, p 34

1. Barbican,	2. Gatehouse
3. Curtain wall	4. Drawbridge
5. Moat	6. Arrow loop
7. Crenel	8. Swing shutter
9. Merlon	10. Arrow loops

Pages 35 - 46 See teachers' notes.

A Castle Dictionary, page 47

1. Ashlar	2. bailey
3. battlements	4. garderobes
5. palisade	6. solar
7. wardrobe	8. seneschal
9. chaplain	10. almoner
11. steward	12. marshall
13. wardrober	14. page
15. tiltyard	16. war-horse
17. melée	18. tournament
19. joust	20. coat of arms
21. College of Heralds	

A Castle Quiz, page 48
1. A fortified building or a group of fortified buildings.
2. To protect those inside from attack.
3. A fortified Anglo-Saxon township.
4. A man-made mound of earth on which a keep was built.
5. The courtyard of a castle and its surrounding buildings. (Also called a ward.)
6. A stronghold with an earth mound on which was a wooden or stone keep surrounded by a ditch and fortified enclosure or courtyard.
7. The main tower of a medieval castle.
8. The principal room in a keep, used for main meals, receiving guests and for entertainment.
9. A building placed in front of a keep often containing the entrance to it.
10. A wooden fence built as a first line of defence against attack.
11. A shell keep.
12. A connecting wall joining the towers of a castle.
13. Concentric castles.
14. (a) A deep water-filled or earth-filled ditch surrounding a castle.
    (b) A moveable bridge which could be raised or lowered from inside the castle.
15. A strong wooden or iron grilled gate used to block the entrance to a castle. It was set in grooves so that it could slide up and down.
16. The well-defended entrance to the stronghold.
17. Two gatehouses were usual at this time.
18. An outwork from which the gateway or entrance to a castle was defended.
19. Literally murder holes, holes in the ceilings of a castle for dropping sand, stones, boiling liquids . . . on those below.
20. Garderobes.
21. (a) A small private chapel.
    (b) A stone wash-basin fixed against a wall.
    (c) A private living room.
22. Machicolation.
23. A narrow opening in the castle wall through which arrows or missiles were fired.
24. The postern.
25. An observation hole in the wall of a room, often used to see what is going on in another room
26. A master mason.
27. Master James of St. George. A Savoyard.
28. (a) A loose top-coat decorated with insignia.
    (b) The respective colours and designs of a particular King, baron or knight.
29. The seneschal or steward of the lands.
30. The wardrober or treasurer.

ANSWERS

Page 49

In the Middle Ages, boys from noble families often trained to become knights. A young boy started his apprenticeship as a page. Later he became a squire. Knights practised their skills in a special area called a tiltyard. The knight rode at a special target, the quintain and tried to hit it with his lance. The target was weighted so that it swung back and hit any careless or untrained rider. Knights also practised by fighting each other in mock duels. Sometimes these jousts were held in front of a crowd for entertainment at a tournament. Each knight rode a war horse and wore chain mail or a suit of armour. So that he could be identified, a knight wore a coat of arms which bore the badges or insignia of his master.

Page 51

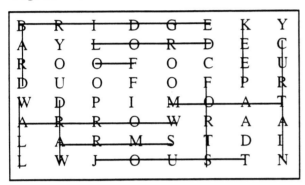

1. WE ARE BESIEGED.
   PLEASE SEND HELP.

   R DROO HVMW URUGB
   PMRTSGH ZG LMXV.

3. Motte, keep, bailey, curtain wall,
   gatehouse, barbican, murder holes,
   portcullis, loop, moat.

Castle Maths, p 50

1. Vol. = $\frac{22}{7}$ (9² - 4·5²) x 21 m³

   = 4000·9 m³

2. Number of stones
   = $\frac{2 \times 22 \times 9 \times 100 \times 21 \times 100}{7 \times 20 \times 30}$

   = 19,800

3. Cost = £600 (23,000 + 80,000)
   = £61·8 million

RECORD SHEET
CASTLES

Name _____ Age_____

Page	Master Copy
29	A Castle
30	Early Castles
31	Inside a Keep
32	A Twelfth Century Castle
33	A Barbican and Gatehouse
34	Defensive Structures
35	A Knight
36	Design a Coat of Arms
37	Jousting
38	A Castle Plan
39	A Castle under Attack
40	Defending a Castle
41	Prisoners and Torture
42	A Castle Feast
43	Food and Cooking
44	The Castle Times
45	Historical Sources
46	Everyday Life in a Castle
47	A Castle Dictionary
48	A Castle Quiz
49	A Castle Frieze
49	A Cloze Test
50	Castle Maths
51	Puzzles
52	Castle Game
53	Project Ideas

BOOKLIST

GENERAL REFERENCE BOOKS/PUBLICATIONS

Bagley, J. J.	*Historical Interpretation: the Sources of English History 1066 - 1540*, Harmondswoth, 1965
Betjeman, J.	*A Pictorial History of English Architecture*, Murray, 1972
Briggs, A.	*A Social History of England*, Weidenfeld and Nicholson, 1983
Blyth, J.	*History in Primary Schools*, Open University Press, 1989
Burke, G.	*Towns in the Making*, Edward Arnold, 1971
Cheney, C. R. (ed.)	*Handbook of Dates*, Royal Historical Society, 1945
Collier, W.	*Historic Buildings*, Spurbooks, 1973
Contamine, P.	*War in the Middle Ages*, (English translation), Blackwell, 1984
Fossier, C. (ed.)	*The Cambridge Illustrated History of the Middle Ages, 1250 - 1520*, CUP, 1986
Greeves, L.	*The National Trust Atlas*, George Philip, 1981
Hallam, E.	*The Plantagenet Chronicles*, Tiger, 1995
Harrison, M.	*Homes in History*, Wayland, 1983
Labarge, M.W.	*A Baronial Household in the Thirteenth Century*, Harvester, 1980
Little V and John, T	*Historical Fiction in the Classroom*, Historical Association, 1986
Maurois, A.	*An Illustrated History of England*, Viking Press (New York), 1964
Powicke, F. M. (ed.)	*Handbook of British Chronology*, Royal Historical Society, 1939
Strickland, M.	*War and Chivalry*, CUP, 1996
Warren, W.I.	*Henry II*, Eyre Methen, 1973

Clark, G. (ed.)	*The Oxford History of England*, OUP, various dates (several volumes are useful)
Stenton, Sir F.	*Anglo-Saxon England c550 - 1087*
Poole, A. L.	*From Domesday Book to Magna Carta, 1087 - 1216*
Powicke, Sir M..	*The Thirteenth Century, 1216 - 1307*
McKisack, M.	*The Fourteenth Century, 1307 - 99*
Jacob, E. F.	*The Fifteenth Century, 1399 - 1485*
Mackie, J. D.	*The Earlier Tudors, 1485 - 1558*

The Dictionary of National Biography (obtainable at most public libraries)
Guide to the Manuscripts Preserved in the Public Record Office, HMSO (latest edition)
The Last Two Million Years, Readers' Digest Association, 1973
Treasures of Britain, Drive Publications and the AA, 1972

The Victorian History of the Counties of England (has commentaries on the history of each parish)

ANNUAL PUBLICATIONS

Museums and Galleries (in the United Kingdom), Johansens.
Historic Houses, Castles and Gardens, Johansens.
Historic House Directory, Norman Hudson and Co., Banbury

WALES

Davies, W.	*Wales in the Early Middle Ages*, Leicester University Press, 1982
Dodd. H.	*A Short History of Wales*, Batsford, 1977
Lloyd, J. E.	*A History of Wales from the Earliest Times to the Edwardian Conquest*, 2 vols. , Longman Green, 1911
Roderick, A. J. (ed.)	*Wales Through the Ages*, 2 vols., C. Davies, 1960
Williams, D.	*A History of Modern Wales*, John Murray, 1950, revised by J.E. Jones, 1977
Williams, G. A.	*When Was Wales?* Penguin, 1991

BOOKS ON CASTLES

Armitage, E. S.	*The Early Norman Castles of the British Isles*, CUP, 1912
Brown, R. A.	*English Castles*, 3rd. ed., Macmillan, 1976
Cormick, P.	*Castles of Britain*, Peerage Books, 1982
Colvin, H.M. (ed.)	*A History of the King's Works*, vols 1-2, HMSO, 1913
Hewitt, H. J.	*The Organisation of War under Edward III*, Manchester University Press, 1966
Keen, M.H.	*The Laws of War in the Late Middle Ages*, OUP, 1965
Leask, H. G.	*Irish Castles and Castellated Houses*, OUP, 1941
Mackenzie, W. M.	*The Medieval Castle in Scotland*, Batsford, 1927
Oman, C.	*History of the Art of War in the Middle Ages*, OUP, 1911. Revised by J. H. Beeler, 1953
Platt, C.	*The Castle in Medieval England and Wales*, Dent, 1982
Robinson, D. M and Thomas, R.	*Wales: Castles and Historic Places*, HMSO, 1990
Simpson, W. D.	*Castles in England and Wales*, Batsford, 1969

Singer, C.	*The History of Technology*, OUP, 1954
Toy, S.	*The Castles of Great Britain*, 2nd. ed., CUP, 1954
Toy, S.	*A History of Fortification from 3000 BC to AD 1700*, CUP, 1955
White, L.	*Medieval Technology and Social Change*, OUP, 1962

The National Trust, The National Trust for Scotland, English Heritage and Cadw (Welsh Historic Monuments) publish guide books to individual castles which are excellent. These are illustrated souvenirs with detailed histories of particular castles and an account of what remains today.

Domino Books (Wales) also publish a series of Activity Packs for children on individual castles. The following are available: Beaumaris Castle, Berry Pomeroy Castle, Carew Castle, Chepstow Castle, Cilgerran Castle, Corfe Castle, Llansteffan Castle, Pembroke Castle, Rochester Castle, Upnor Castle, Warwick Castle, Please write for an up to date list.

NOTE A comprehensive list of museums (including some castles) is available in the annual publication, *Museums and Galleries* now published by Johansens. They also publish *Historic Houses, Castles and Gardens* each year.